Measurement in Physical Education and Exercise Science

Volume 1, Number 1, 19

Special Issue:
Measurement, Statistics, and Research Design in Physical
Education and Exercise Science—Current Issues and Trends
Guest Editor: Terry M. Wood

The American Association for Active Lifestyles and Fitness (AAALF) is one of six national associations of the American Alliance for Health, Physical Education, Recreation and Dance (AAHPERD). AAALF's mission is to pursue and promote active lifestyles and fitness through a broad constituency of specialized interest groups, one of which is the Measurement and Evaluation Council. To accomplish its mission, AAALF and its councils focus primarily on four goals—program development and dissemination; research dissemination; leadership; and professional development of its members, including underrepresented groups and issues. This mission perpetuates AAALF's unique historical role of providing resources for and creating linkages among professional organizations inside and outside AAHPERD.

AAALF
1900 Association Drive
Reston, VA 20191–1599
(800) 213-7193
E-mail: aaalf@aahperd.org

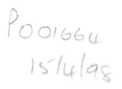

MEASUREMENT IN PHYSICAL EDUCATION AND EXERCISE SCIENCE, *1*(1), 1

EDITOR'S NOTE

Why a measurement journal in physical education and exercise science? All good measurement techniques and tools currently in use within physical education and exercise science ultimately resulted from quality measurement research. The question arose, "Where can measurement research be published?" Although some publications contain information about measurement research, they are very specific to certain content areas. Because most measurement research in physical education and exercise science is based on physical performance data or on data unique to physical education and exercise science, measurement manuscripts are not likely to be accepted for publication in many educational and psychological journals. There weren't enough publishing opportunities for measurement specialists. Further, a journal in which considerable measurement research could be found is definitely needed. So, the reason for a measurement journal in physical education and exercise science is because it is needed.

Measurement in Physical Education and Exercise Science (*MPEES*) evolved over several years through the efforts of many people. Without their efforts, *MPEES* would never have become a reality. Doctoral students David Rowe and Kent Wagoner told me we had to have a measurement journal, and they helped me develop a proposal. Later, doctoral student Scott Murr made many contributions to the proposal. Dr. Janet A. Seaman, executive director of the American Association of Active Lifestyles and Fitness (AAALF), supported *MPEES* in every way possible. Specifically, she secured funds to advertise the new journal and found a publisher for *MPEES*. Drs. Margaret "Jo" Safrit and James Morrow helped develop policies and procedures for *MPEES*. Finally, this inaugural issue of *MPEES* would not be available so soon after it was announced if not for the assistance of Guest Editor Dr. Terry M. Wood.

Ted A. Baumgartner
Editor

MEASUREMENT IN PHYSICAL EDUCATION AND EXERCISE SCIENCE, *1*(1), 3
Copyright © 1997, Lawrence Erlbaum Associates, Inc.

GUEST EDITOR'S NOTE

This inaugural issue of *Measurement in Physical Education and Exercise Science* is devoted to exploring measurement, research design, and statistics issues in six subdisciplines of exercise and sport science. All articles in this issue were invited papers presented at the 8th Measurement and Evaluation Symposium, *Exploring the Kaleidoscope* (October 24 to 26, 1996, Oregon State University, Corvallis).

The symposium brought together nationally and internationally renowned measurement specialists and content experts to discuss issues related to measurement, research design, and statistics. The following articles thus reflect some of the best thinking concerning these issues in our discipline.

In the first article, Richard J. Stiggins (subdiscipline: pedagogy) outlines standards of assessment quality for physical educators and eloquently addresses the dilemma of providing adequate assessment without adequate resources. Next, Robert W. Christina (motor learning/control) and Diane L. Gill (sport and exercise psychology) examine the importance of properly conceptualizing and defining the appropriate research questions as the "source and solution" for measurement and design issues in their respective fields of study. C. Roger James and Barry T. Bates (biomechanics) and Marcel Bouffard (movement studies in disability) then make the case for the study of individuals (e.g., single-subject and other small-sample designs) in contrast to the more traditional study of groups. The last article, by Zung Vu Tran (exercise physiology), focuses on the importance of computing and reporting statistical power in research. Tran provides simple power and sample-size tables for repeated-measures analysis of variance.

We hope you enjoy these articles. To the extent that they raise more questions and invite new solutions, this issue will be judged a success.

Terry M. Wood
Guest Editor

MEASUREMENT IN PHYSICAL EDUCATION AND EXERCISE SCIENCE, *1*(1), 5–17

Dealing With the Practical Matter of Quality Performance Assessment

Richard J. Stiggins

Assessment Training Institute
Portland, Oregon

Recently, as I departed from an elementary school after presenting an after-school workshop on assessment, Jason—one of the participating teachers—called to me from across the parking lot to raise a follow-up issue. He apologized for delaying my return home but said that it was an issue he just couldn't raise during the session. Jay faced a troubling dilemma and, frankly, didn't want the others to know that he didn't know how to handle it—especially his supervisor, who also participated in the workshop. Here is Jay's description of the problem:

> I am the physical education [PE] teacher for three different elementary schools. I spend part of each day in each school. My job is to take over for the regular classroom teacher for PE instruction. Each teacher delivers her or his charges to me for 40 minutes, I engage them in the activities I have planned for the period, and then the students return to their regular classroom. Every class period everyday, I face a new group of students. So every week, I see several hundred students—none for more than a few minutes.
>
> Now here's my dilemma: At report card time every 10 weeks, I am required to enter a grade for each student. The district provides me with a list of names of my students, and I am supposed to evaluate each of them. They expect me to differentiate between and among them and assign grades as appropriate. But as I read down page after page of names, I don't even know three quarters of these kids by name! And even if I did, there is no way I could take time to assess their physical education achievement one by one—accu-

---

Requests for reprints should be sent to Richard J. Stiggins, Assessment Training Institute, Suite 300, 50 SW 2nd Avenue, Portland, OR 97204. E-mail: 73704.2432@compuserve.com.

rately or inaccurately. There are just too many of them and too little time. So, I complained to my supervisor, who advised me, just grade them on their effort. But if I don't know who they are, how can I do even that? No one could get to know and assess this number of students. This is a joke—a game we play to try to make kids behave, and parents believe we have standards in PE. What should I do?

Jay and his physical education colleagues are not the only teachers facing this dilemma. Music, art, and other service teachers are forced to deal with this same set of circumstances regarding report-card grading. How should they address their assessment and reporting responsibilities?

As it turns out, this question has concrete answers, although some will find the answers unsatisfying. Possible solutions become more and more clear the higher one's level of assessment literacy—that is, the more informed one is about the differences between sound and unsound assessment and grading practices. These circumstances stymie Jason because they present him with a series of immovable barriers to quality assessment and effective communication. Removal of those barriers will take specific action related to grading policy and practice. The path to resolution, however, will remain a mystery to those who are unschooled in the basic principles of sound classroom assessment.

This article spells out a set of commonsense standards of assessment quality that, if met in any assessment context, will maximize the accuracy of the information we generate about student achievement. Jay's circumstances precluded him from meeting these standards. Let's see why.

FIVE STANDARDS OF ASSESSMENT QUALITY

Here I briefly describe the keys to sound assessment. Then I explore how each plays out in Jason's classroom.

Standard 1: Quality assessments arise from and accurately reflect clearly specified and appropriate achievement expectations for students. As educators, we must begin the assessment process with a sharply focused vision of the achievement we expect of our students, because different achievement targets require the application of different assessment methods. In any assessment context, we must begin assessment development with a clear vision of what it means for our students to succeed. Do we expect our students to:

1. Master (i.e., *know and understand*) a subject? (Does this mean that they must know it outright, or does it mean that they must know where and how to find it using references?)

2. Use knowledge to *reason* and solve problems?
3. Demonstrate mastery of specific *performance skills*—where it is the doing that is important?
4. Use their knowledge, reasoning, and performance skills to create *products* that meet standards of quality?

Because there is no single assessment method capable of assessing all of these various forms of achievement, one cannot select a proper method without a focused sense of which of these expectations are to be assessed. Jay would be prepared to assess for grading if he had determined in advance which of the four kinds of achievement just listed he expects his students to attain.

Standard 2: Sound assessments are designed to serve prespecified instructional purposes.   We cannot design assessments without asking who will use the results and how they will use them. Because different users need different information in different forms at different times to fulfill their decision-making responsibilities, there is no single assessment that can meet everyone's needs.

Table 1 lists the important users of assessment in schools. Each user needs different information to answer different questions. To provide quality information for teacher, student, and parent use at the classroom level, we need high-quality classroom assessments; to provide useful information for policy or instructional support, we need quality standardized tests. Because of the differences in information needs, we must begin each assessment event with a clear sense of whose needs we are meeting. Otherwise, our assessments are without purpose.

In Jay's case, the publicly stated purpose for his assessments is to assign report-card grades. This means that he strives to communicate to students and parents how each student is doing in meeting the academic standards in physical education class. To make Jay's report-card grades interpretable, then, both he (the message sender) and his students and their parents (both message receivers) need to know and understand what forms of achievement are to be factored into the grade symbols used (A, B, C, etc.).

Standard 3: High-quality assessments use methods that accurately reflect the intended target and serve the intended purpose.   As teachers often have several different kinds of achievement to assess, and as no single assessment method can reflect them all, we must rely on a variety of methods. The options include selected-response tests (multiple choice, true–false, matching, fill-in), essay tests, performance assessments (based on observation and judgment), and assessments based on direct personal communication with the student (oral examinations,

TABLE 1
TABLE 1
Users and Uses of Assessment Results

Users	Key Question(s) to Be Answered	Information Needed
Classroom Level		
Student	Am I meeting the teacher's standards? What help do I need to succeed? Are the results worth my investment of energy?	Continuous information about individual student attainment of specific instructional requirements
Teacher	Which students need what help? Who among my students should work together? What grade should appear in the report card?	Continuous information about individual student achievement
	Did my teaching strategies work? How do I become a better teacher?	Continuous assessment of group performance
Parent	Is my child succeeding in school? What does my child need to succeed? Is my child's teacher(s) doing the job? Are educators in this district doing a good job?	Continuous feedback on their child's mastery of required material
Instructional Support Level		
Principal/ vice-principal	Is instruction in particular areas producing results? Is this teacher effective? What kinds of professional development will help? How shall we spend building resources to be effective?	Periodic assessment of group achievement
Supervising teacher or department chair	What does this teacher need to do the job?	Periodic assessment of group achievement
Counselor/ psychologist	Who needs (can have access to) special support services such as remedial programs? Which students should be assigned to which teachers in order to optimize results?	Periodic assessment of individual achievement
Curriculum director	Is our program of instruction effective?	Periodic assessment of group achievement

(Continued)

TABLE 1 *(Continued)*

Users	Key Question(s) to Be Answered	Information Needed
Policy Level		
Superintendent	Are programs producing student learning? Is the building principal producing results? Which programs need/deserve more resources?	Periodic assessment of group attainment of district curriculum
School board	Are students in the district learning? Is the superintendent producing results?	Periodic assessment of group achievement
State department of education	Are programs across the state producing results?	Periodic assessment of group attainment of state curriculum
Citizen/legislator (state or national)	Are students in our schools achieving in ways that will allow them to be effective citizens?	Periodic assessment of group attainment of valued targets

Note. From *Student-Centered Classroom Assessment, 2nd Edition* (pp. 26–28), by Richard J. Stiggins, 1977, Upper Saddle River, NJ: Prentice-Hall. Copyright © 1997 by Prentice-Hall. Adapted by permission of Prentice-Hall. (Book is distributed to Practicing teachers and administrators by the Assessment Training Institute, Portland, OR.)

interviews, discussions, etc.). Our assessment challenge is to know how to match the assessment method with an intended achievement target, as depicted in Table 2. Our professional development challenge is to be sure that all concerned with quality assessment know and understand how the various pieces of this puzzle fit together.

Therefore, in Jay's physical education classroom, the methods he chooses to track the achievement of his students must be a function of his achievement expectations. Some targets—like health knowledge or understanding of the rules of a game—might translate into relatively efficient paper-and-pencil assessment methods. But, how would he administer these in the gym? Further, it is likely that Jay would need to rely on performance assessments of skills to be demonstrated by students—a labor-intensive enterprise, to say the least.

Standard 4: Quality assessments provide a representative sample of student performance that is sufficient in its scope to permit confident conclusions about student achievement. All assessments rely on a relatively small number of exercises to permit the user to draw inferences or conclusions about

TABLE 2
Possible Links Between Achievement Targets and Assessment

	Assessment Method			
Target to Be Assessed	Selected Response	Essay	Performance Assessment	Personal Communication
Knowledge mastery	Multiple-choice, true–false, matching, and fill-in can sample mastery of elements of knowledge	Essay exercises can tap understanding of relations among elements of knowledge	Not a good choice for this target; other three options preferred	Can ask questions, evaluate answers, and infer mastery—but a time-consuming option
Reasoning proficiency	Can assess understanding of basic patterns of reasoning	Written descriptions of complex problem solutions can provide window into reasoning proficiency	Can watch students solve some problems and infer about reasoning proficiency	Can ask student to "think aloud" or can ask follow-up questions to probe reasoning
Skills	Can assess mastery of knowledge prerequisite to skillful performance but cannot rely on this mastery to tap the skill itself	Can assess mastery of knowledge prerequisite to skillful performance but cannot rely on this mastery to tap the skill itself	Can observe and evaluate skills as they are being performed	Strong match when skill is oral communication proficiency; also can assess mastery of knowledge prerequisite to skillful performance
Ability to create products	Can assess mastery of knowledge prerequisite to ability to create quality products but cannot use this mastery to assess quality of products themselves	Can assess mastery of knowledge prerequisite to ability to create quality products but cannot use this mastery to assess quality of products themselves	A strong match can assess (a) proficiency in carrying out steps in product development and (b) attributes of product itself	Can probe procedural knowledge and knowledge of attributes of quality products but not product quality

Note. From *Student-Centered Classroom Assessment, 2nd Edition* (p. 81), by Richard J. Stiggins, 1997, Upper Saddle River, NJ: Prentice-Hall. Copyright © 1997 by Prentice-Hall. Adapted by permission of Prentice-Hall. (Book is distributed to practicing teachers and administrators by the Assessment Training Institute, Portland, OR.)

a student's mastery of larger domains of achievement. A sound assessment offers a representative sample of all those possibilities that is large enough to yield confident inferences about how the respondent would have done if given all possible exercises. Each assessment context places its own special constraints on our sampling procedures. Our quality-control challenge is to know how to adjust the sampling strategies to produce results of maximum quality at minimum cost in time and effort.

To meet this standard, Jay must plan carefully and take time to sample the performance skills of each of his students. Only then can he draw defensible conclusions about the extent to which each student has met his grading standards.

Standard 5: Sound assessments are designed, developed, and used in such a manner as to eliminate sources of bias or distortion that interfere with the accuracy of results.   Even if we devise clear achievement targets, transform them into proper assessment methods, and sample student performance appropriately, there are still factors that can result in an assessment score misrepresenting a student's real achievement. Problems can arise from the test, the student, or the environment in which the test is administered. Our challenge is to be aware of the potential sources of bias and distortion, as listed in Table 3, and to know how to devise assessments, prepare students, and plan assessment environments to deflect these problems before they affect our results.

To assign interpretable grades reflective of each student's achievement, Jay must develop and conduct his assessments in ways that systematically preclude bias due to these factors. If circumstances prevent him from doing so, there is a very real danger of mismeasurement and the assignment of unusable, uninterpretable report-card grades.

Summarizing Standards of Excellence in Assessment

To develop a quality assessment environment, teachers and administrators must first understand these five standards and know how to implement them in each assessment they develop and conduct. Table 3 highlights these quality criteria.

TABLE 3
Standards of Assessment Quality

Standard	*Quality Control Question*
Clear targets	Is the nature of the achievement to be demonstrated clear?
Clear purpose	Has the user and use of assessment results been made clear?
Proper method	Can the assessment method used properly reflect the intended target?
Sound sample	Have just enough exercises been devised for students to show what they can do without spending too much time?
Bias controlled	Have all relevant sources of bias been accounted for and eliminated in assessment design and use?

ANALYZING JAY'S DILEMMA

Is Jay right in contending that the report-card grading policies to which he must adhere are a "joke"—part of an illusion intended to make it appear that standards of academic rigor are being applied? Let's see—one standard of quality at a time.

Standard 1: Clear and appropriate achievement targets. This should not present a problem for Jay. Any teacher in any classroom context should be prepared to define the achievement targets expected of students. In fact, sound practice would suggest that the entire health and physical education faculty should meet across grade levels within the district to (a) formulate a vision of what they expect successful graduates of their instructional program to know and be able to do by the end of high school, (b) systematically divide up responsibility across grade levels for the attainment of those targets, and (c) make sure each and every teacher is a confident, competent master of the targets that are her or his instructional responsibility.

When this is done, Jay knows and understands what knowledge his students are to master, how they are expected to use that knowledge to reason and solve problems, and what performance skills they are to be able to demonstrate. These, then, would serve as the basis for Jay's grades. If these targets have not been articulated, however, sound assessment and grading will remain beyond reach.

Standard 2: Clear reasons for assessing. Again, we find little reason to be concerned about Jay's situation. He is expected to assess for the purpose of assigning grades. He is prepared to deliver on this responsibility when he begins the grading period with a clear set of achievement expectations, a manageable assessment plan for documenting how each student has done in meeting those grading standards, and a way to keep records of student achievement. Jay is set to reach his grading goal of communicating with students and parents about their performance in his classes when he is prepared to assess, record, and summarize prespecified achievement in a careful manner.

Standard 3: Appropriate assessment methods. On its face, this standard seems to present no problem. For each kind of target, Table 2 reveals viable assessment methods. All Jay needs to do is select methods consistent with his targets. However, upon further analysis, it becomes clear that this standard and the two standards that follow—all of which relate to how Jay must measure student achievement in health and physical education—capture the heart of his problem.

Assuming that Jay wants his students to master a subject (perhaps health and physical well-being), he can turn to selected-response assessment methods. But, several questions arise immediately, given his responsibilities. Are these appropriate for primary-grade students who have yet to develop test-taking skills? For older students, is Jay to administer tests to several hundred students at once? If he does, how shall he score them, record the results, and keep accurate records of each student's performance for later grading purposes? How shall he handle the information-management challenges? If the answer is by computer, who will provide the hardware, software, and training needed to implement these systems?

Assuming that Jay expects his students to be able to use this knowledge to reason and solve real-world personal health and physical well-being problems that might come up in their lives—authentic problems—what methods is he to use? If he chooses selected-response methods, all of the questions raised in the previous paragraph become relevant here too. If he chooses performance assessments, then the list of questions grows. Let's examine how.

Assuming that Jay wants his charges to develop some performance skills—that is, the ability to do certain things of a physical nature—he has no choice but to turn to performance assessment. These assessments evaluate student achievement by means of observation and judgment. To make this work, Jay must align performance exercises with his achievement expectations, devise and train himself to apply performance criteria reflective of those expectations, and set up recording methods capable of maintaining profiles of his judgments of student proficiency. This represents a considerable workload all by itself, and we have yet to begin the observation-and-evaluation process itself—for several hundred students. How is Jay to accomplish all of this and teach too?

Standard 4: Appropriate sample.   If any test is a sample of all of the questions a teacher could have asked but didn't have time for, then Jay could sample the knowledge and reasoning achievement of his students quite efficiently using machine-scored, selected-response tests (at least for those old enough to take such tests).

But what about sampling with respect to performance skills using performance assessments? These require one-on-one observation and professional judgment, which means that Jay must devise enough performance exercises in order to provide a representative sample of each student's proficiency for each performance skill, and administer them to each student individually in order to conduct systematic observation and recording of results.

Sampling errors can occur when we oversample or undersample performance. Oversampling wastes time. We spend too much time gathering too much data for the target. In short, the assessment process reaches a point of diminishing returns. Jay is unlikely to commit this kind of error.

Undersampling produces insufficient evidence of proficiency to permit teachers to draw confident conclusions. The assessment results are too thin to produce confident generalization. Exercises might fail to reflect the broad array of performance possibilities. Or, students might get to demonstrate proficiency too few times to show what they really can do. Under his current circumstances, Jay is almost certainly doomed to commit this kind of sampling error when assessing student mastery of performance skills.

Standard 5: Reducing bias and distortion.   Faced with the challenge of assessing several hundred students' mastery of knowledge, reasoning, and skill achievement, Jay could succumb to any of the various sources of bias and distortion listed in Table 4. The scope of the assessment process itself, combined with the pace at which Jay would need to conduct it, could give rise to:

1. Bias within the assessment itself, as in the case of exercises insensitive to the unique personal, gender, cultural, or ethnic backgrounds of the students, most of whom Jay does not know.
2. Bias within Jay, the performance rater, who would face the fatigue of systematically rating the achievement of several hundred students.
3. Bias within the student, as in the case of frustration due to delays in being assessed or cheating due to potential lack of supervision during assessment.
4. Bias within the environment in which the assessments might take place—such as distractions due to the hectic nature of the assessment process.

And this is just the beginning of the list.

A Summary of Jay's Plight

In this context, circumstances make it impossible for the teacher to conduct the high-quality assessments needed to generate the accurate achievement records needed to produce report-card grades reflective of actual student achievement. In fact, Jay is doomed—as he readily admits—to assign meaningless grades in terms of what students have learned. Given the resources available, he is unable to meet the five key assessment-quality standards that form the foundation of accurate assessment and meaningful grades.

Clearly, Jay can and should work with his colleagues to articulate clear and appropriate targets; he can focus sharply on his grading purpose; and he can even identify proper assessment methods given his expectations. However, due to the demands of his teaching context, Jay still might not be able to sample student

TABLE 4
Some Examples of Potential Problems in Assessing Accurately

Problems Common to All Methods	Problems Unique to Each Format
Potential problems that can occur within the student:	
Lack of reading skill	Possible problems with multiple-choice tests:
Language barriers	More than one correct response
Emotional upset	Incorrect scoring key
Poor health	Incorrect bubbling on answer sheet
Physical handicap	Clues to the answer in the item or in other items
Peer pressure to mislead assessor	
Lack of motivation at time of assessment	Problems with essay assessments:
Lack of testwiseness (understanding how to take tests)	Student lacks writing skill
Lack of personal confidence leading to evaluation anxiety	No scoring criteria
	Inappropriate scoring criteria
	Evaluator untrained in applying scoring criteria
Possible problems that can occur within the assessment context:	Bias due to stereotypic thinking
Noise distractions	Insufficient time or patience to read and score carefully
Poor lighting	
Discomfort	Potential problems with performance assessment:
Lack of rapport with assessor	No scoring criteria
Cultural insensitivity in assessor or assessment	Inappropriate scoring criteria
Lack of proper equipment	Evaluator untrained in applying scoring criteria
	Bias due to stereotypic thinking
Examples of problems that arise from the assessment itself (regardless of method):	Insufficient time or patience to observe and score carefully
Directions lacking or vague	
Poorly worded questions	
Poor reproduction of test questions	Possible difficulties when using personal communication:
	Inadequate sampling of performance
	Problems with inaccurate record keeping

performance in a bias-free, distortion-free manner to produce accurate information about the achievement of each individual student.

Resolving Jay's Problem

What, therefore, should Jay do? One course of action might be to follow his supervisor's advice and grade on something other than achievement, such as student effort—how hard students tried to learn or perform. But, if Jay has difficulty accurately assessing the achievement of his students because of their huge numbers and the need to rely on labor-intensive assessment methods, how does it help to change the student characteristic to be assessed?

Both Jay and his supervisor must realize that, just because we change from an achievement target to an affective target, we do not get to abandon our standards of assessment quality. Jay would need to:

1. Clearly and specifically define what it means to put forth effort such that the target is within reach of all students.
2. Translate that definition into appropriate assessment methods (and the range of available methods remains the same).
3. Sample the performance of each individual student in ways that lead to confident conclusions about how hard each student tried.
4. Avoid all relevant sources of bias and distortion that can arise in the assessment of student effort.

Thus, this does not seem to represent a viable solution.

In fact, there are only two courses of action left that have any hope of solving Jay's dilemma. The first is to give him a viable assessment-and-grading task. Make the task feasible—either (a) reduce his teacher–student ratio to a point at which systematic high-quality assessment is feasible or (b) bring sufficient support personnel into the assessment process to help Jay do it right.

The second possible course of action is to abandon this unworkable grading policy. Health and physical education, art, music, and other service teachers who face hundreds of students each week are not able to accurately assess any student characteristics (be they achievement or affect) in bias-free, distortion-free ways. Sooner or later, instructional leaders, policymakers, and communities must face this reality. We either acknowledge that this challenge is insurmountable and change the grading policy, or we give Jay and his colleagues the tools and other resources needed to do the job.

Working with grading policies that promote the appearance of academic rigor and quality assessment—while in fact abandoning standards of assessment quality—places students directly in harm's way and falls far short of the need to conduct fair and accurate assessments of student achievement and performance mastery.

We need to look critically at the quality of our assessment practices and adhere rigorously to these key standards of quality.

REFERENCES

Stiggins, R. J. (1997). *Student-Centered Classroom Assessment, 2nd Edition.* Upper Saddle River, NJ: Prentice-Hall. (Distributed by the Assessment Training Institute, Portland, OR)

MEASUREMENT IN PHYSICAL EDUCATION AND EXERCISE SCIENCE, *1*(1), 19–38

Concerns and Issues in Studying and Assessing Motor Learning

Robert W. Christina

School of Health and Human Performance
University of North Carolina at Greensboro

Lest this introduction be wasted on remarks of little value, suffice it to say that this article focuses on selected concerns and issues commonly encountered when we attempt to study and assess motor learning. The crux of the problem is that, at present, motor learning cannot be directly observed and measured; it must be inferred from motor performance, which can be directly observed and measured. Thus, learning and performance are not the same, and performance might or might not be an index of learning. For instance, all changes in performance during acquisition do not reflect learning, and the absence of changes in performance during acquisition do not necessarily indicate that learning has not occurred. Thus, the basic challenge we face in studying motor learning is to provide convincing evidence that the changes observed in motor performance can be attributed solely to learning.

This article begins with an overview of how we define motor learning because our definition determines, to a great extent, how we study and assess it. Next, it addresses several concerns about how some scholars have approached the study of motor learning. Then it discusses measurement and experimental design issues and difficulties typically encountered when we attempt to provide convincing evidence to support the position that the performance changes observed are due to learning. It concludes with recommendations for studying and assessing motor learning.

HOW MOTOR LEARNING IS DEFINED

Overview

Scholars' respective definitions and explanations of human motor learning can be found in several textbooks and are not repeated here. For illustrative purposes,

---

Requests for reprints should be sent to Robert W. Christina, Office of the Dean, School of Health and Human Performance, 401 HHP Building, University of North Carolina, Greensboro, NC 27412–5001. E-mail: christin@iris.uncg.edu.

however, the following two definitions are presented as representative examples. Magill (1993) defined motor learning as "a change in the capability of a person to perform a skill that must be inferred from a relatively permanent improvement in performance as a result of practice or experience" (p. 44). Schmidt (1988) preferred to write that "motor learning is a set of processes associated with practice or experience leading to relatively permanent changes in the capability for responding" (p. 346). These two definitions and the others reviewed vary mainly because it is difficult to formulate a satisfactory statement that includes everything we would like to include and excludes everything we would like to exclude. Interestingly, however, the various definitions have not been a major source of controversy in the field largely because the differences among them are few in number and are usually resolved through discussion in which the meanings of the terms at the heart of the differences are provided.

Generally, all of the definitions reviewed distinguish between (a) the types of changes with associated antecedents that qualify as motor learning and (b) the related types of changes with associated antecedents that do not qualify as motor learning. Specifically, the three major elements common to the reviewed definitions are that (a) motor learning is a process or set of processes by which the capability for performance is changed relatively permanently, (b) motor learning is not directly observable, and (c) motor learning is inferred from a relatively permanent change in performance produced by practice or experience rather than by factors that do not qualify as learning, such as maturation or temporary states of the individual (e.g., fatigue, drugs, motivation). These elements along with the particular problem to be investigated influence how we study and assess motor learning. Essentially, these elements require that our experimental design and method of measurement demonstrate a relatively permanent change in performance as a result of practice to be able to infer that motor learning has occurred.

Concerns

One concern with the definitions that make a relatively permanent change in performance the only prerequisite for making an inference about motor learning is that they guide us toward measuring the product or outcome of learning (i.e., motor task performance) and not how the outcome is represented and how the associated processes operate to produce the outcome. Product-oriented definitions concentrate on what motor task is learned and tend to neglect how it comes about—that is, how the motor task is represented and how the associated processes operate to produce it. Product-oriented definitions capture a static view of learning that is, in fact, dynamic in nature. The static view is quite different from the dynamic view emphasizing the importance of changes in the representational structure for a task.

The dynamic view holds that performance capability reflects available task properties along with the processes used to operate on them. For example, based on one well-known perspective (Schmidt, 1988), task properties might consist of the motor program and associated parameters necessary for performance. In addition, it is likely that the processing structure by which task properties are acquired is also learned during practice. This processing structure can be used for memory-retrieval purposes by assisting in the reconstruction of forgotten task properties when attempts at direct retrieval fail. Such reconstructive retrieval is characteristic of retention for even the most simple motor task (see Logan, 1988).

The problem is that we are still using product-oriented definitions to guide our measurement of motor learning, but we are asking process-oriented research questions. Product-oriented definitions were used when the stimulus–response (S–R) or product-oriented research approach was popular. The shift in our field from the S–R approach to the information-processing approach probably began in the late 1960s, growing in strength in the 1970s and 1980s (Christina, 1987). In the 1990s, we are deeply entrenched in process-oriented research, but we are using product-oriented definitions that are not capable of helping us answer process-oriented questions about motor learning. Process-oriented research is attempting to help us gain a more complete understanding of (a) what was learned in acquisition, (b) how "the learning" itself was represented, and (c) how "the learning" is used (i.e., the processes involved) to produce skillful motor performance. What is needed is a definition of motor learning that will help us gain this understanding by guiding us toward experimental designs, procedures, and measures of other aspects of performance in addition to "relative permanent changes." This definition should capture more of a dynamic (process and product) rather than static (product) perspective of motor learning. In the absence of such a definition, however, we should be creative in our use of the product-oriented definitions available and interpret them in ways that enable us to study the dynamic nature of motor learning.

Another concern with the definitions reviewed is that they are provisional in nature and not formally satisfactory due to the number of their terms that are not operationally defined. For example, a difficulty with all definitions that make a relatively permanent change in performance a prerequisite for making an inference about motor learning is that the phrase relatively permanent is vague. How the phrase is operationally defined is quite arbitrary and varies across studies. Although a standardized operational definition of the phrase would erase this difficulty, developing it would be a major undertaking that might be unrealistic. However, it would not be unrealistic to develop an operational definition of the phrase relatively permanent that could be consistently used across studies investigating the same motor-learning problem. This would offer at least a basic level of formalization and standardization that would allow for comparison of results across studies.

APPROACHES TO THE STUDY OF MOTOR LEARNING

Traditional Approach

Despite the definitional concerns such as the two just outlined, motor learning has been and continues to be meaningfully studied, usually by employing the following six steps:

1. Define a dependent variable that can be reliably observed and that is a movement performance appropriate for studying the problem.
2. Define at least one independent variable appropriate for studying the problem that can be reliably manipulated and that is thought to influence motor learning.
3. Design learning opportunities in which the defined movement performance (dependent variable) occurs under the conditions defined by the independent variable.
4. Observe changes in the defined movement performance.
5. Exclude changes in the defined movement performance that are a function of nonlearning factors such as maturation or temporary states of the individual (e.g., motivation, fatigue, drugs).
6. Make an inference about motor learning as a function of the independent variable manipulated if the change in the defined movement performance is relatively permanent and the result of practice.

These six steps are based on the well-known "scientific method" and on how we define motor learning. It is easy to recognize how the three major elements common to most definitions of motor learning manifest themselves in the six steps.

Problem- Versus Method-Oriented Approaches

One concern with how we approach the study of motor learning involves researchers who restrict their investigation of motor-learning problems to one particular method of assessment because that is the only method they know. These researchers are method-oriented because their method—whether it be a certain experimental design, statistical analysis, or measurement technique—determines the population of problems that they can study. Such scholars are restricted to conducting motor-learning research on problems that can be studied by their particular method. One resulting effect is that many important motor-learning problems that fall outside the boundaries of their method are not studied. Another effect is that problems that need to be studied using more than one method (disciplinary or interdisciplinary) are studied with a single method that can provide only restricted information about the solutions. This method-oriented approach has impeded the development of motor-learning knowledge. How we assess motor learning, first and foremost, should be a function of the problem we wish to study. This is a problem-oriented approach. It requires us to be willing to put aside our favorite method and learn the methods that are most appropriate for studying the problem. If the methods cannot be learned in a reasonable amount of time, we should join forces with other researchers who know them even if these researchers are from other disciplines (e.g., measurement, biomechanics). In so doing, we will be able to go beyond the boundaries of any one method of assessment and reach freely toward motor-learning problems that are the most important to study and examine them more thoroughly.

Doctrine-of-Disproof Approach

The study of some problems will demand descriptive methods because they are applied or atheoretical in nature. Other problems will require the inferential methods that are characteristic of hypothesis testing and theory testing in science. When inferential methods are used, we often are not as rigorous as we should be in adhering to the *doctrine of disproof,* which holds that science advances only through disproofs (Kuhn, 1962; Popper, 1959). If motor learning is to advance significantly as a field of science, this doctrine must be consistently and rigorously applied. The doctrine demands systematic application of the method of inductive inference to every motor-learning problem studied by using the following steps described by Platt (1964):

1. Formulate alternative hypotheses.
2. Design one or more decisive experiments with alternative outcomes, each of which will exclude at least one hypothesis.
3. Conduct each experiment so as to obtain an unambiguous result.
4. Repeat Steps 1 to 3 to refine the remaining possibilities ... and so on.

My years of research experience in the field of motor learning have led me to the conclusion that we can do much better at systematically applying the steps of the method of inductive inference. Those of us unfamiliar with these steps can begin by learning them; then we can become proficient at using them by rigorously applying them to every motor-learning problem studied. Once we understand the steps, we should teach them to our students. Those of us who already know the steps but who have been inconsistent or less than rigorous in applying them, simply need to change how we do business; we must become more consistent and rigorous in applying them not only to our own problems, but to problems studied by others as well.

One very simple aid that can be used to effectively apply the steps of the method of inductive inference is Platt's (1964) "the Question." Platt suggested that each proposed hypothesis should be met with the question "What experiment could disprove this hypothesis?" and that each description of an experiment should be met with the question "What hypothesis does this experiment disprove?" The Question goes straight to the heart of whether or not we are effectively applying the steps of the method of inductive inference and adhering to the doctrine of disproof. It directs us to concentrate on whether we are or are not taking a testable scientific step forward.

Cooperative Approach Between Basic and Applied Research

Christina (1987, 1989) presented a three-level approach for studying motor-learning problems. Essentially, the three levels range from the most basic to the most applied research on human motor learning divided according to relevance for providing solutions to practical problems. The ultimate goal of basic (Level 1) research is to develop theory-based knowledge appropriate for understanding the learning of many different motor skills in a variety of settings, but with no requirement to demonstrate the value of the knowledge for solving practical problems. Typically, Level 1 research tests hypotheses in laboratory settings using experimenter-designed motor tasks that often have little or no relevance to the kinds of motor skills performed in the real world.

The goal of Level 2 research is to develop theory-based knowledge appropriate for understanding the learning of practical motor skills in practical settings, but with no requirement to find immediate solutions to practical learning problems. Level 2 research tests hypotheses in a practical setting or in a laboratory setting similar to the practical setting of interest and employs real-world motor skills or experimenter-designed motor skills that have the properties of real-world skills. Level 2 research strives to develop a body of scientific knowledge directed toward specific practical needs. For instance, it could focus on developing theory-based knowledge appropriate for understanding the learning of sport skills in sport settings, but with no requirement to find immediate solutions to sport problems. Such specialized knowledge could provide a much needed rational basis for the profession of physical education or coaching. Specialized knowledge generated at Level 2 is usually applicable to fewer situations than the fundamental knowledge produced at Level 1 because it is constrained by the practical needs of the particular profession or technology it serves.

The main goal of applied (Level 3) research is to find immediate solutions to practical motor-learning problems, but with no requirement to demonstrate the value of these solutions to the development of theory-based knowledge at either Level 1 or 2. Level 3 research tests solutions to practical motor-learning problems described under Level 2.

Research at Levels 2 and 3 is suppressed by the view we adopted to guide our motor-learning efforts during the past three decades. Essentially, this view held that applied research at Level 2 or 3 is an extension of, is subordinate to, and is almost completely dependent on basic research at Level 1. More specifically, applied research at Level 3 was seen as nothing more than application of theory-based knowledge derived from basic research to the solution of practical problems, and applied research at Level 2 was seen as the building of a specialized body of knowledge derived from the fundamental knowledge of basic research. Because both types of applied research relied heavily on the use of theory-based knowledge of basic research at Level 1, they were considered an extension of basic research. Further, because our current body of theory-based knowledge of motor learning was less than adequately developed to be used for applied research, a concerted effort to conduct applied research at Levels 2 and 3 was viewed as a highly questionable endeavor.

This view biased us into thinking that applied research at both Levels 2 and 3 is subordinate to and almost completely dependent on basic research at Level 1 and has very little if anything to contribute to basic research. Allowing this kind of thinking to guide our research efforts these past three decades, we suppressed applied research at Levels 2 and 3 and isolated it from basic research at Level 1. This is truly unfortunate because, by suppressing applied research at Levels 2 and 3, we not only ignored its potential for helping practitioners find solutions to their practical problems, but we overlooked the special potential it has for assisting basic research in its attempt to build a body of theory-based motor-learning knowledge. Further, isolating applied research from basic research is unfortunate because mechanisms of motor learning and theory and research in the basic processes are intimately related to the applied aspects of learning motor skills in practical and real-world settings.

Clearly, the time has come for us to change the view that has been guiding our research efforts in motor learning. Instead of thinking of applied research at Levels 2 and 3 as an extension of basic research at Level 1, we should think of them as independent but cooperating endeavors that have a synergistic relation. This alternative view not only acknowledges that research at Levels 2 and 3 can be an extension of basic research, as it is under the current view, but it also recognizes that applied research can take place independently of basic research. Moreover, the alternative view holds that research at Level 2 or 3 can contribute to the ultimate goal of basic research just as basic research can contribute to the ultimate goals of research at Levels 2 and 3.

In areas in which theory-based knowledge from basic research is sufficiently developed, we can determine the appropriateness of applying that knowledge to practical settings through research at Levels 2 and 3. However, some of us fail to realize that specialized knowledge can be developed solely by Level 2 research in areas in which the theory-based knowledge of basic (Level 1) research is not adequately advanced. Likewise, there is no reason why immediate solutions to our practical problems cannot be found solely by Level 2 research when the theory-based knowledge of basic (Level 1) research (or even the specialized knowledge of Level 2 research) is not sufficiently developed.

If we are fortunate enough to develop a new idea or hypothesis or to discover some new information from our research at either Level 2 or 3, the contribution to fundamental motor-learning knowledge can be evaluated by subjecting the development or discovery to the rigor of controlled laboratory testing of basic (Level 1) research. In this way, applied research at Levels 2 and 3 can contribute to basic research. Thus, it is clear that, when we view research at Levels 1, 2, and 3 as independent but cooperating endeavors, the three levels have the potential to contribute to one another. This is a much more viable and promising approach for us to adopt to guide our future research efforts than the one that holds that applied research at Levels 2 and 3 is an extension of basic research.

ASSESSING MOTOR LEARNING IN ACQUISITION

Perhaps the most common way of examining performance changes as a function of practice trials in acquisition is a learning curve (which more accurately should be termed a *performance curve* to maintain the learning–performance distinction). The performance curve tells us something relatively special about performance changes in the dependent measure under the conditions defined by the independent variable—something from which an inference about learning can be made. However, before an inference is justified, (a) one must rule out all explanations that would attribute the performance change observed in the curve to variables that do not qualify as motor learning (e.g., maturation or temporary states of the individual caused by factors such as motivation, fatigue, drugs), and (b) one must be able to advance the explanation that the changes were relatively permanent and a function of practice. Important to the assessment of motor learning in the acquisition phase is determining when training or practice is complete. It is usually considered complete when a defined performance level or mastery criterion is achieved. Although it has been traditional to speak of the level of performance in acquisition as the level of original learning, the *level of performance in acquisition* is preferred as a more correct expression because it maintains the learning–performance distinction.

How the performance level or mastery criterion is selected (i.e., how it is defined and assessed in terms of when it is satisfactorily achieved) is quite arbitrary. The level or criterion is usually measured in terms of trials needed, time required, or frequency of errors made until it has been achieved. Achieving a mastery criterion set at a level demanding somewhat stable performance over many practice trials may be interpreted as evidence of a relatively permanent change in performance, provided that temporary performance effects can be ruled out. In most studies reviewed, however, the criterion has been established either at a minimal level of mastery (e.g., the first trial performed without error) or at a slightly more than minimal level (e.g., three successive trials performed without error). In addition to setting an arbitrary criterion of mastery, the slope of the curve in acquisition could be used to determine when performance has stabilized at or above the criterion level (Jones, 1985). When the slope has begun to plateau at or above the criterion level of mastery, acquisition is considered complete. Another way to assess the level of performance in acquisition is by using a dual-task paradigm to determine the degree of automaticity of performance (for a discussion of this approach, see Schmidt, 1988). Using this paradigm, a secondary task is given to subjects to sample their cognitive capacity while they are acquiring the primary task. The point at which neither of the tasks causes a performance decrement on the other is considered an acceptable degree of automaticity and thus an acceptable level of performance. Although this paradigm can be an effective way of assessing the degree of automaticity, it too is not without problems.

Clearly, the arbitrary nature of the mastery criterion makes it difficult if not impossible to perform certain comparisons across studies because the criterion varies from study to study. It depends on how the criterion of mastery in acquisition is defined and on how it is quantified in terms of when learning is judged to be complete. These complications notwithstanding, the mastery criterion continues to be used to study learning in the acquisition phase. Moreover, the consistent use of the same mastery criterion across studies investigating the same motor-learning problem would make it possible to conduct meaningful comparisons across studies. Of course, the use of any performance measure obtained in acquisition could be contaminated with temporary performance effects caused by independent variables (e.g., knowledge of results, distribution of practice) manipulated in acquisition such that the measure might not reflect learning. If temporary performance-effect contamination is suspected in the planning of the study, it must be dealt with in a reasonable way, which typically involves an experimental design that allows for the assessment of performance in postacquisition using retention or transfer tests. I address this later in this article.

One major problem assessing motor learning in acquisition is that the performance changes observed in acquisition might or might not reflect learning. Some training procedures known to enhance performance during acquisition might or might not enhance learning; conversely, other training procedures that introduce difficulties (e.g., contextual interference) for the learner and that impair performance during acquisition might in fact foster learning (see Schmidt & Bjork, 1991, for some examples). In short, the goal of training in acquisition is to optimize learning, which, based on our current definitions, is some relatively permanent change in the capacity for performing that must be inferred from a somewhat permanent change in performance due to practice or experience. What is observed during acquisition is performance localized in a given place and time. At a later time, in another place, the learner might perform quite differently, and that performance is often at an inadequate level. The performance observed during acquisition might be mediated by training variables that produce a temporary effect rather than a relatively permanent effect indicative of learning. As the performance level or mastery criterion achieved in acquisition might or might not be an accurate indicator of motor learning, it is important also to assess performance in postacquisition with retention and/or transfer tests.

ASSESSING MOTOR LEARNING IN POSTACQUISITION

Retention Tests

Motor learning is assessed in the postacquisition phase with a retention design and test mainly (a) to determine the durability or relative permanence of the level of performance achieved in acquisition over longer periods of disuse than could have been demonstrated in acquisition and (b) to determine if the level of performance in acquisition is temporary and due to variables that do not qualify as learning, or if it is relatively permanent and the result of practice as well as other variables manipulated that do qualify as learning.

When studying retention, traditionally a distinction is made between the acquisition and retention phases of the experiment. The acquisition phase involves the time or trials required to attain a certain level of task proficiency. The retention phase follows the acquisition phase and a retention interval (i.e., time period of nonuse or no practice) that might vary from being short (e.g., seconds or minutes) to long (e.g., weeks, months, or years). The retention phase usually consists of a test to determine how much of the task proficiency attained during the acquisition phase is retained or, alternatively, how many trials are saved in relearning the task that was originally learned in the acquisition phase. Thus, it is common to use the term *retention* when performance on the task practiced during the acquisition phase is assessed in the retention phase under conditions that are essentially the same as those that existed in the acquisition phase. The term *transfer* is used when the task and/or conditions present in the retention phase differ from those that existed in the acquisition phase.

For the purposes of this article, the common usage of these two terms is followed, but it is important to understand the concept that retention so defined is actually a special case of transfer. Retention and transfer are related in the sense that the postacquisition context can differ from the acquisition context along the dimensions of time and overall similarity. These dimensions are related in that, with the passage of time over the retention interval, the acquisition and postacquisition contexts tend to become less similar because the mechanisms that affect the emotional, physical, and cognitive states of the performer are operating. For example, the mechanisms that produce forgetting or that change one's motivation to perform operate during the retention interval. In this sense, a retention test can be interpreted as a test of the transfer of learning to contexts that appear to match the context of the acquisition phase (Christina & Bjork, 1991).

Although retention designs, tests, and measures to assess motor learning are very helpful, they must be used wisely and in conjunction with performance measures recorded in acquisition. A detailed description of several issues and concerns surrounding the use of retention measures and tests to assess motor learning appears in two previous articles (Christina & Shea, 1988, 1993) and is not repeated here. However, I discuss four issues or concerns because they are central to this article.

Maintaining the learning–retention distinction.   When we measure motor performance in the acquisition phase, we are studying the learning or acquisition of a defined performance. However, when we measure motor performance in the retention phase, we are studying the persistence of the acquired defined performance over time. Some researchers (e.g., Lee & Genovese, 1988) have made the mistake of thinking that retention-performance measures are measures of motor learning when in fact they are indirect measures of the retention of motor learning. Performance measures in acquisition are used to make inferences about mechanisms, processes, and outcomes of motor learning, whereas performance measures in retention are used to make inferences about memory mechanisms and forgetting processes that operate during the retention interval to affect what is learned in acquisition.

When we use a retention test or measure to assess the relative permanence of the motor learning that occurs in acquisition, care must be taken through our design and procedures to control or account for the effects due to factors such as warm-up, motivation, and forgetting that could operate during the retention interval to affect measures taken on retention tests. For example, longer retention intervals would allow for more of the massed practice effects that temporarily depress performance in acquisition to dissipate and thus make absolute retention scores less contaminated by these effects. At the same time, however, longer retention intervals could increase the decrement in performance measured on the retention test caused by forgetting or by not warming up or could produce an increment in performance due to increased motivation. The use of retention tests to assess the relative permanence of motor learning could confound the amount learned in acquisition with these factors if they operate over the retention interval and if our experimental design and procedures do not control or account for their effects (for a more detailed discussion, see Christina & Shea, 1988).

Assessing motor learning based on restricted information.   Christina and Shea (1988) argued that making a practice of reducing the assessment of motor learning to one retention measure (e.g., absolute retention score), as Lee and Genovese (1988) did, can produce misleading inferences about motor learning. This is especially the case if a perspective is taken that emphasizes the complexity of memory representation. From this perspective, we are better able to assess the effects of different variables on the constructs underlying learning and retention as more rather than less performance information is known. Christina and Shea argued that the various retention measures (e.g., relative retention score, percent relative retention, absolute retention score, final score) provide specific information about a particular aspect of performance that the other measures are incapable of providing. Each measure tells something different about performance from which a relatively unique inference about learning can be made. However, when considered together, the different types of information provided by the various measures complement one another and fit together like the pieces of a puzzle to provide a more complete picture about the effects of an independent variable on performance and learning. Selecting only one of these types of information on which to base an inference about learning, as Lee and Genovese did by using the absolute retention score, is analogous to looking at one piece of a puzzle to determine what the entire picture looks like. The danger in using this approach is that the score selected reflects some but not all of the performance information that performers have produced. Thus, performance information is lost, and the inference made about the effect of an independent variable on motor learning is based on a limited amount of information.

Christina and Shea (1993) extended the argument by making a case for studying relearning so that a savings score could be used in conjunction with an absolute retention score to provide a more comprehensive assessment of the memory constructs underlying the retention of motor learning. Relearning following a retention interval as a way to assess retention actually consists of two components—a *first-trial recall score* and a *savings score.* The first-trial recall score, also referred to as the *absolute retention score,* is the level of performance on the initial trial of the retention test. The absolute retention score is supposed to reflect the amount retained of what was originally learned in acquisition. The savings score is the number of trials required for subjects to reach the level of mastery they achieved in acquisition. Interestingly, there appears to be no consistent or definable relation between these two scores. In fact, based on an extensive literature review, Adams (1987) concluded that "forgetting of procedural responses can be complete in about a year, although there are savings because relearning is rapid" (p.54). Thus, subjects might show little or no retention in their absolute retention score on the first relearning trial but might demonstrate in their savings score a substantial savings in the number of trials in relearning. In this situation, the absolute retention score appears to tell us that nothing was retained, but the savings score suggests that something was retained—or, from a representational perspective, the absolute retention score tells us that the task properties were no longer available, but the savings score tells us that the processing structure was differentially intact or more suitable for the testing context. It is obvious that, if the absolute retention score is used alone, the conclusion reached would be quite different than if both scores are used.

In summary, we are better able to assess the relative permanence of motor learning by using more rather than less performance information. Each of the measures used provides us with information about a particular aspect of performance that the other measures are incapable of providing. When considered conjointly, however, the different types of information generated by the various measures complement one another and fit together like pieces of a puzzle to provide a more complete picture about the relative permanence of motor learning.

Incomplete understanding of the measures used.   It is not uncommon to find results based on different retention measures (e.g., absolute retention score, percent relative retention, relative retention score, final score) that appear to be in conflict and lead to divergent inferences about the retention of motor learning (i.e., the relative permanence of motor learning). For example, retention can be measured with an absolute retention score or a relative retention score. Absolute retention is the level of performance on the initial trial(s) of the retention test. Relative retention can be either (a) a difference score that represents the amount of loss in acquired performance over the retention interval or (b) a percentage score that represents the amount of loss in performance over the retention interval relative to the amount of performance improvement shown in acquisition (i.e., original learning). If forgetting is measured by either of the relative retention scores, relative retention decreases with increases in the amount of original learning. However, if forgetting is measured by an absolute retention score, then absolute retention increases with increases in the amount of original learning. As Schmidt (1988) pointed out, "Thus, the statement of a law relating retention of skills to the amount of original practice is completely different depending on how retention is measured" (p. 497). Schmidt's position was reinforced by Lee and Genovese (1988).

Christina and Shea (1988) argued that the results appear to be in conflict and lead to divergent conclusions only because Schmidt (1988) and Lee and Genovese (1988) compared scores reflecting different aspects of performance without a thorough understanding of the nature of these differences. Schmidt and Lee and Genovese simply failed to recognize that the three scores measure different aspects of performance. The problem here was not with these scores, but with the misinterpretation of what they actually represent. For example, Schmidt and Lee and Genovese failed to recognize that neither the relative retention score nor the percent relative retention score qualify as direct measures of retention (i.e., performance aspects that are retained). Only the absolute retention score reflects the amount of performance retained after the retention interval. When the measures are interpreted for what they actually reflect, the results are not in conflict and do not lead to divergent conclusions. For instance, Bourne and Archer's (1956) data reveal that longer intertrial intervals in acquisition (i.e., more distributed practice) produce higher absolute retention scores and lower relative retention scores. Expressing these results in terms that describe what the scores actually represent, we find that longer intertrial intervals in acquisition produce the greatest amount of performance retained after the retention interval and the least amount of performance change (i.e., lost) over the retention interval from the end of acquisition. If percent relative retention scores are used, then longer intertrial intervals produced the least change (i.e., loss) over the retention interval in the amount of performance improvement observed in acquisition. Bourne and Archer's data also reveal that the shorter intertrial intervals (i.e., more massing of practice) produced higher relative retention scores and lower absolute retention scores. When these results are stated in terms that describe what the scores actually reflect, it becomes clear that the shortest intertrial intervals resulted in the least amount of performance retained after the retention interval and the greatest amount of performance change (i.e., lost) over the retention interval from the end of acquisition. If percent relative retention scores are employed, then the shortest intertrial intervals produced the greatest change (i.e., loss) over the retention interval in the amount of performance improvement seen in acquisition. Together, these three scores seem to provide nonconflicting, converging lines of evidence to support the conclusion that longer intertrial intervals result in better retention than shorter intertrial intervals.

Clearly, each of these scores provides information about a particular aspect of performance that the other scores are incapable of providing. The key to successful use of these and other scores is (a) knowing what aspect of performance each of the scores reflects, (b) having a thorough understanding of the interrelations among the different scores, and (c) understanding the methodological and measurement problems inherent in each of the scores. Such understanding will lead to more purposive selection among the scores for a particular study and will provide a basis for interpreting the results obtained in various studies using different scores.

A case for using immediate and delayed retention tests.   Scores such as relative retention scores that make use of performance measures obtained from acquisition data might be contaminated with temporary effects caused by independent variables being manipulated in acquisition (e.g., massed practice) such that they might not reflect learning. Some have assumed that these effects are present only when the independent variables are present. However, temporary performance effects can persist and be present well after the independent variables are removed, as pointed out by Christina and Shea (1988).

In some situations, the presence of temporary performance effects can be assessed reasonably well by the administration of both immediate and delayed retention tests (Christina & Shea, 1993). In the case of an immediate retention test, the retention interval should be the same as the intertrial interval during the acquisition phase of the experiment. For both the immediate and delayed retention tests, the acquisition groups should be tested under the same experimental conditions. A more definitive description of temporary performance effects might be obtained if conditions were included in the experimental design in which the independent variable (e.g., knowledge of results) was left intact for the retention tests. Presumably, temporary performance effects would still be present for the immediate retention test for all conditions, but would have the opportunity to dissipate by the time of the delayed retention test. This would especially be the case for the conditions in which the independent variable of interest was removed for the retention tests.

There is at least one other reason for including both immediate and delayed retention tests in the study of motor learning. Comparison of performance between these tests can be informative about whether knowledge of task properties was acquired during practice or forgotten during the retention interval. Such a determination can have important implications for theoretical explanations concerning the operation of learning variables (see Christina & Shea, 1993, for examples and discussion).

Transfer Tests

Motor learning is assessed in the postacquisition phase with a transfer design and test mainly (a) to determine if the performance changes observed in acquisition are temporary and due to variables that do not qualify as learning, or if they are relatively permanent and the result of practice as well as other variables manipulated that do qualify as learning, (b) to determine the direction of transfer (i.e., if the training in acquisition produced motor learning that enhances, impedes, or has no effect on performance in the postacquisition context), and (c) to determine the generalization of transfer (i.e., the extent to which training in acquisition produced a level of motor learning that prepares people to perform in a postacquisition context that differs from the acquisition context). Transfer designs, tests, and measures to assess motor learning are very helpful, but they should be used wisely and in conjunction with performance measures recorded in acquisition. Although there are many issues and concerns that could be addressed, covering all of them in this article is prohibitive. However, I address two issues or concerns because they are especially relevant to the focus of this article.

Separating temporary from relatively permanent effects.   One common way to determine if the performance changes observed in acquisition are temporary or relatively permanent is to use an experimental design that allows for the assessment of performance in postacquisition using a transfer test. The ideal way to accomplish this is to use a complete transfer design in which all the tests and necessary control and experimental groups are included in both the acquisition and transfer phases. The double-transfer design recommended by Dunham (1971, 1976) is an example of this complete design approach. In the acquisition phase of a practice distribution experiment, for instance, two groups of subjects (say, Groups 1 & 2) experience distributed practice, and two groups (Groups 3 & 4) experience massed practice; in the transfer phase, Group 1 continues distributed practice, Group 2 shifts to massed practice, Group 3 continues massed practice, and Group 4 shifts to distributed practice.

Compared to incomplete transfer designs, a complete design puts us in a better position to make an inference about the effect of massed and distributed practice on motor learning. The complete design enables us to separate relatively permanent performance changes that we can attribute to learning from temporary changes caused by variables that do not qualify as learning (i.e., effect of switching conditions and massed practice). In spite of the great value of a complete design such as the double-transfer design, quite often incomplete designs are used (e.g., Stelmach, 1969) because they "cost" less in terms of number of subjects and amount of time needed to conduct the research. However, what we save in terms of this cost might not be worth what we lose in terms of scientific benefit. Conversely, this cost might not be worth what we gain in terms of scientific benefit. Whenever faced with a decision about whether to use a complete or incomplete design, we would be wise to ask whether the experimental design we have selected adheres to the doctrine of disproof. If we think it does, we should be able to answer the Question, "What hypothesis does this experimental design disprove?"

Problems in measuring transfer effects.   Like the measurement of retention effects, the measurement of transfer effects has been plagued by several problems. First, transfer has been measured using different formulae across studies, which can produce different results (see Cormier & Hagman, 1987). Before the results and conclusions reached in different studies are compared, one must be certain that the same formula was used to measure the effects of transfer.

Second, it is essential to know the type of transfer performance being measured from one study to the next. For instance, were transfer effects assessed by performance on the first trial of the transfer task or by performance reflecting the overall rate of learning the transfer task? Typically, the purpose of the study determines which performance measure is selected to assess transfer. The measure selected will constrain the results and conclusions. This must be taken into consideration when comparing studies that used different performance measures to assess transfer effects.

Third, the reliability and validity of experimental- and control-group performance need to be evaluated in order to make relative comparisons from transfer performance across studies. Questions that should be asked, for example, are whether the level of performance mastery in acquisition was the same for both groups, whether ceiling effects masked the level of original learning after performance reached the maximum on the dependent measure, whether the sample size was adequate, whether there was a sufficient amount of practice in original learning, and whether there were any floor effects. A thorough treatment of each of these problems in assessing transfer of learning is beyond the scope of this article, but the interested reader is referred to Cormier and Hagman (1987) and Schmidt (1988) for detailed discussions of these and other sources of measurement error.

Fourth, the real-world environment frequently makes it difficult to carry out appropriate transfer methods and paradigms in spite of their validity. As a result, the findings and conclusions of applied research need to be subjected to careful examination because they might be (to some degree) a function of the operational constraints imposed by the real-world environment.

In summary, the different methods of measuring transfer effects, like those used to measure retention effects, have problems associated with them that can influence the validity of the conclusions that are reached not only within a given study but across studies as well. Some have argued that a meta-analysis should be applied to the existing literature on retention and transfer, but this does not appear to be an appropriate solution for at least two reasons, according to Jackson (1980). First, using a meta-analysis to infer which features of studies on a particular subject determined the discrepant findings is not advisable. Second, using a meta-analysis when the metrics for the dependent measures used in the various studies on a subject are not standard or equivalent does not seem to be appropriate. For example, what is the common metric across studies measuring the criterion of mastery or level of original learning; retention; rate of forgetting; and amount of transfer? Is learning a list of paired English and German nouns to the first completely errorless trial equivalent to performing a motor task to the first completely errorless trial? Obviously, these questions have no simple answers. It also seems that much of the literature suffers from at least two major limitations—a situation that would have to be overcome to justify the use of the meta-analysis approach inappropriate.

RECOMMENDATIONS FOR STUDYING AND ASSESSING MOTOR LEARNING

In this article, I have addressed some concerns, difficulties, and issues typically encountered when one attempts to study and assess motor learning. They arise mainly because we cannot measure motor learning directly and must make inferences about motor learning based on measures that directly assess the relative permanence of motor performance. In spite of this complication, motor learning has been and will continue to be meaningfully studied and assessed, especially if the following recommendations are followed:

1. The definition of motor learning on which we base our research should be selected with the understanding that it will influence how we study and assess motor learning. If we are interested in conducting research on the outcomes of motor learning, then our traditional product-oriented definitions are appropriate for use. However, if our research is process-oriented, we must go beyond the boundaries of product-oriented definitions and assess other aspects of performance that reflect the dynamic nature of learning in addition to "relatively permanent changes," which tend to focus on the outcome and static nature of learning.

2. A problem-oriented rather than method-oriented approach should be adopted to study motor learning because it enables us to go beyond the boundaries of any one method of assessment and reach freely to conduct more thorough research on problems that are most important to investigate.

3. The doctrine of disproof must be more consistently and rigorously applied to our inferential research if motor learning is to advance appreciably as a field of science.

4. The approach that views basic and applied research as independent but cooperating endeavors—rather than applied research solely as an extension of basic research—is recommended if motor learning is to develop a comprehensive body of knowledge that is enriched with relevance.

5. When a criterion of mastery is used to assess motor learning in acquisition, it is recommended that the criterion be set at a level that demands somewhat stable performance over as many practice trials as are needed to qualify as one line of evidence indicating that a relatively permanent change in performance due to practice has occurred.

6. Consistent use of the same criterion of mastery across studies investigating the same motor-learning problem is recommended if we wish to make comparisons across studies.

7. Because the criterion of mastery achieved in acquisition might or might not be an accurate indicator of motor learning, additional evidence should be obtained by assessing performance in postacquisition with retention and/or transfer tests.

8. Retention tests should be used to determine (a) relative permanence of the level of performance achieved in acquisition over longer periods of disuse than could have been demonstrated in acquisition and (b) whether the level of performance achieved in acquisition is temporary or relatively permanent.

9. When retention tests are used to assess the relative permanence of motor learning, care must be taken to control or account for effects due to factors (e.g., warm-up, motivation, forgetting) that could operate during the retention interval.

10. Inferences about motor learning should not be based on a single score but on more rather than less performance information. Performance scores or measures that provide us with different types of information about acquisition and retention/transfer in postacquisition should be considered together when making our inferences.

11. In certain situations, immediate and delayed retention tests might be appropriate for assessing the presence of temporary performance effects and forgetting over the retention interval.

12. Transfer tests should be used to determine (a) whether the level of performance achieved in acquisition is temporary or relatively permanent and (b) the direction and generalization of transfer.

13. When faced with a decision about whether to use a complete or incomplete transfer design as a basis for making an inference about motor learning, we should ask if the experimental design adheres to the doctrine of disproof. If it does, we should be able to identify at least one hypothesis that the design disproves.

REFERENCES

Adams, J. (1987). Historical review and appraisal of research on the learning, retention, and transfer of human motor skills. *Psychological Bulletin, 101,* 41–74.

Bourne, I., Jr., & Archer, E. (1956). Time continuously on target as a function of distribution of practice. *Journal of Experimental Psychology, 51,* 25–32.

Christina, R. (1987). Motor learning: Future lines of research. In M. Safrit & H. Eckert (Eds.), *The academy papers: The cutting edge in physical education and exercise science research* (pp. 26–41). Champaign, IL: Human Kinetics.

Christina, R. (1989). Whatever happened to applied research in motor learning? In J. Skinner, C. Corbin, D. Landers, P. Martin, & C. Wells (Eds.), *Future directions in exercise and sport science research* (pp. 411–422). Champaign, IL: Human Kinetics.

Christina, R., & Bjork, R. (1991). Optimizing long-term retention and transfer. In D. Druckman & R. Bjork (Eds.), *In the mind's eye: Enhancing human performance* (pp. 23–56). Washington, DC: National Academy Press.

Christina R., & Shea, J. (1988). The limitations of generalization based on restricted information. *Research Quarterly for Exercise and Sport, 59,* 291–297.

Christina, R., & Shea, J. (1993). More on assessing the retention of motor learning based on restricted information. *Research Quarterly for Exercise and Sport, 64,* 217–222.

Cormier, S., & Hagman, J. (Eds.) (1987). *Transfer of learning: Contemporary research and applications.* New York: Academic.

Dunham, P. (1971). Learning and performance. *Research Quarterly, 42,* 334–337.

Dunham, P. (1976). Distribution of practice as a factor affecting learning and/or performance. *Journal of Motor Behavior, 8,* 305–307.

Jackson, G. (1980). Methods for integrative reviews. *Review of Educational Research, 50,* 438–460.

Jones, M. (1985). *Nonimposed overpractice and skill retention* (Tech. Rep. No. 86–55). Alexandria, VA: Army Research Institute for the Behavioral and Social Sciences.

Kuhn, T. (1962). *The structure of scientific revolutions.* Chicago: University of Chicago Press.

Lee, T., & Genovese, E. (1988). Distribution of practice in motor skill acquisition: Learning and performance effects reconsidered: *Research Quarterly for Exercise and Sport, 59,* 277–287.

Logan, G. (1988). Toward an instance theory of automatization. *Psychological Review, 95,* 492–527.

Magill, R. (1993). *Motor learning: Concepts and applications* (4th ed.). Dubuque, IA: Brown.

Platt, J. (1964). Strong inference. *Science, 146,* 347–352.

Popper, K. (1959). *The logic of scientific discovery.* New York: Basic.

Schmidt, R. (1988). *Motor control and learning: A behavioral emphasis* (2nd ed.). Champaign, IL: Human Kinetics.

Schmidt, R., & Bjork, R. (1991). New conceptualizations of practice: Common principles in three paradigms suggest new concepts for training. *Psychological Science, 3,* 207–217.

Stelmach, G. (1969). Efficiency of motor learning as a function of intertrial rest. *Research Quarterly, 40,* 198–202.

MEASUREMENT IN PHYSICAL EDUCATION AND EXERCISE SCIENCE, *1*(1), 39–53

Measurement, Statistics, and Research Design Issues in Sport and Exercise Psychology

Diane L. Gill

Department of Exercise and Sport Science
University of North Carolina at Greensboro

To identify measurement, statistics, and design issues is a formal way of asking, "How do we answer our research questions?" Before addressing that question, however, we must first ask, "What are our research questions?" As a specialist in sport and exercise psychology, I interpret my main task as identifying the research questions and content issues of sport and exercise psychology. If content specialists can accomplish that task, then the measurement specialists can work with the content experts to answer those questions.

The theme that continues throughout this article is the one take-home, bottom-line message for both sport and exercise psychology scholars and our measurement colleagues: Identifying our research questions, or achieving conceptual clarity, is the source and solution for our measurement, statistics, and design issues. When research has a clear purpose and conceptual framework, when constructs are clearly defined, and when clear and relevant questions are asked, we solve many problems. Moreover, we get better advice when we ask the experts.

My favorite research advice comes from Lewis Carroll's (1865/1992) *Alice's Adventures in Wonderland.* Alice (the searching researcher) asks Cheshire-Puss (the resident measurement expert) for advice, "Would you tell me, please, which way I ought to walk from here?" Cheshire-Puss returns the question (as do all expert advisors): "That depends a good deal on where you want to get to." When Alice replies that she doesn't much care where, the sage responds, "Then, it doesn't matter which way you walk." If we cannot tell our advisors where we want to get to, we cannot expect them to tell us how to get there.

Requests for reprints should be sent to Diane L. Gill, Department of Exercise and Sport Science, University of North Carolina, Greensboro, NC 27412. E-mail: diane_gill@uncg.edu.

THE CONTENT OF SPORT AND
EXERCISE PSYCHOLOGY

Before setting a specific destination of "where we want to get to," let's set a general destination for the content of psychology. Psychology asks many of the same questions asked by other content areas of exercise and sport science and shares many of the same issues. Perhaps the most unique, salient feature of psychology content is the focus on the unobservable—thoughts, feelings, and all the "touchy-feely" things that we cannot really touch and feel. Latent constructs are not merely measurement tools or terms for structural modeling—they are the essence of psychology content.

More formally, most psychology texts define *psychology* as the scientific study of behavior. Thus, we can simply add our context and define *sport and exercise psychology* as the scientific study of behavior in sport and exercise contexts. Although that definition does not seem so latent, as we narrow our path and delve further into the content, we find the ABCs of psychology content: A = affect, B = behavior, and C = cognition. Within psychology, these ABCs—feelings, actions, and thoughts—are all behavior, and behavior is the ultimate outcome for psychology. Psychologists try to understand and explain behavior, as a whole, by looking at the affective, behavioral, and cognitive components and correlates.

A Model for Sport and Exercise Psychology

Sport and exercise psychology researchers focus on holistic behavior rather than on isolated parts of behavior. Within exercise and sport science, psychological research that focuses more on components and processes (e.g., learning and cognitive processing) is done in the area of motor behavior. Sport and exercise psychology specialists typically take a more holistic, social-psychology approach. We try to understand behavior in sport and exercise settings as influenced by individual characteristics (personality, affect, cognitions) and environment (especially social environment—e.g., coaches, group, social culture). The guiding model for sport and exercise psychology is reflected in Kurt Lewin's (1935) classic formula, $B = f(P,E)$, where behavior (B) is a function of person (P) and environment (E).

Measurement, Statistics, and Design in the Psychology Model

Our measurement, statistics, and design issues reflect that dominant model. Measurement issues emphasize personality (P) measures. That emphasis started with the earliest sport psychology research using the personality measures of general psychology, continued with the development of more specific personality or individual-difference measures, and today emphasizes individual dispositions and perceptions related to social-cognitive models (e.g., motivational orientation, perceptions, expectations, attentional style). We do not spend much time on behavior (B) measures, despite their central role in psychology. Sport psychology research typically has defined *behavior* as performance or participation and has increasingly included fitness or health-related outcomes. However, sport and exercise psychologists have left the measurement issues to others. Similarly, sport and exercise psychologists do not spend time on environmental (E) measures. Environmental conditions and variables exist and might be classified, but measurement issues are ignored.

Typical sport and exercise psychology research designs reflect the Lewin model. Sport psychologists might look at the relation of a P variable (e.g., trait anxiety) to a B variable (e.g., performance) or, even more likely, might use factorial models considering the interaction of P and E variables in predicting behavior. For example, a typical research design might examine high- versus low-anxiety persons in competitive versus noncompetitive situations with performance as the dependent variable. Given the typical factorial designs, the logical statistics are analysis of variance, and, often, multivariate analysis of variance (MANOVA). More recently, sport and exercise psychologists have used more continuous P measures with regression analyses as well as MANOVA, but the basic design and statistical models are the same.

Before offering suggestions for advancing beyond this basic model, I review the progress sport psychology has made with measurement, statistics, and design within this framework; highlight some current issues; and discuss directions and options.

PROGRESS IN SPORT AND EXERCISE PSYCHOLOGY MEASUREMENT

From its emergence as an identifiable research specialization in the 1960s, sport and exercise psychology has improved upon measurement, design, and statistical procedures. Some of the advances also apply to other content areas within exercise and sport science, but I focus in this article on progress in measures and research related to individual differences (which, in a measurement sense, is the most notable progress in sport and exercise psychology).

Personality is the first characteristic most people think of when they think of psychology. In fact, personality is one of the earliest topics for sport psychology research. In a recent chapter on measurement in sport psychology, Heil and Henschen (1996) noted the early work with personality measures. They reported that Coleman Griffith (the so-called father of sport psychology) used personality measures and interviewed athletes in the 1930s and 1940s. They did not mention, but other sources (e.g., Gould & Pick, 1995) have indicated, that Griffith also used many laboratory tests and measures (e.g., reaction time, motor coordination, attention) to assess athletes and took a more scientific and broader view of sport behavior than was implied in Heil and Henschen's chapter. But, as Heil and Henschen noted, personality measures dominated early work and hit a peak (or valley, depending on the viewpoint) around 1969 with the popular but psychometrically unsound Athletic Motivation Inventory (Tutko, Lyon, & Ogilvie, 1969). Since 1969, sport psychology has gradually moved away from global personality measures to more specific measures.

Sport-Specific Measures

One of the most important advances for sport psychology measurement was the evolution from general personality measures to sport-specific measures of individual differences relevant to sport and exercise behavior. Martens's (1975) development of the Sport Competition Anxiety Test (SCAT) initiated the move to sport-specific measures. Martens drew upon related theoretical and empirical work on anxiety to develop a model of competitive anxiety, reasoning that a sport competition–specific measure would better identify individuals who become anxious in competition than would more general anxiety measures. The SCAT was developed following appropriate psychometric standards of test development and validation.

Other sport and exercise psychologists followed Martens's (1975) example to develop other sport-specific instruments to measure relevant individual differences. Carron, Widmeyer, and Brawley (1985) developed the Group Environment Questionnaire (GEQ) to measure cohesion. Gill and Deeter (1988) developed a sport-specific measure of competitive achievement orientation, Sport Orientation Questionnaire (SOQ), and subsequent sport anxiety measures have improved on the SCAT.

Multidimensional Measures

Many of the most important constructs of sport and exercise psychology are multidimensional, and recently we have used multidimensional conceptual frameworks and measurement procedures to develop appropriate multidimensional measures. For example, anxiety is now conceptualized and examined as a multidimensional construct, usually with cognitive anxiety/worry and somatic anxiety/physiological arousal dimensions. Smith, Smoll, and Schutz (1990) developed the Sport Anxiety Scale (SAS) with cognitive, somatic, and distraction dimensions. Like the SCAT, the SAS assesses individual differences in the tendency to become anxious in sport, but the SAS likely will replace the unidimensional SCAT in research and applications based on multidimensional approaches to sport anxiety.

States and Traits

The issue of state and trait measures is related. Personality typically implies trait measures—that is, measures of enduring dispositions that reflect a tendency to behave in a given way (e.g., anxious) consistently. Personality states are more immediate; a person might be in a state of high anxiety at a particular time but might not necessarily have high trait anxiety. Personality theories assume that traits are related to states. For example, the high–trait-anxious person tends to have high state anxiety more often than a low–trait-anxious person. However, states are also affected by situation. Anxiety research, in particular, differentiates states and traits, and our measures reflect that differentiation. For example, Martens, Vealey, and Burton (1990) developed the multidimensional Competitive State Anxiety Inventory–2 (CSAI–2), now widely used in sport psychology research and practice.

Perceptions and Cognitions

In moving away from global personality, sport psychology also moved away from personality dispositions (although not entirely) to emphasize more immediate perceptions and cognitions. This work reflects the strong social-cognitive movement in psychology through the 1980s, and sport and exercise psychology has adopted that approach with related models and measures. Within that general social-cognitive approach, sport and exercise psychologists have investigated and measured attributions, expectations, self-perceptions, and, particularly, self-efficacy. Because these constructs relate to an immediate situation, they are measured for that immediate situation, and we do not have standard measures with established reliability and validity, introducing some measurement issues.

For example, self-efficacy is particularly popular and useful in research and practice. Self-efficacy is the belief that one has the capability of successfully performing a task or behavior. Bandura (1977, 1986) offered guidelines for measures. Most measures are similar, asking respondents to rate how confident they are that they can perform a specific task (e.g., finish a 10K run in 35 min) on a scale ranging from 0% (*not at all confident*) to 100% (*absolutely certain*). However, the specific referent tasks are not standard, and researchers seldom pilot measures or check reliability or validity in any way.

Bandura's (1977, 1986) model suggests three dimensions of efficacy—strength (represented by the percent scale), level (a hierarchy of tasks), and generality (the extent that efficacy generalizes to related tasks). Yet, we seldom assess those dimensions or consider the theoretical underpinnings when developing measures. More often, simple scales and items are developed for a particular study, used with little if any pilot testing, and interpreted as though they were valid measures of particular social-cognitive constructs.

Measures of Affect and Emotion

Sport and exercise psychologists have been studying and measuring anxiety, an emotion, for some time. More recently, psychology has seen a reemergence of the broader area of emotion and affect. Conceptual models of emotion call for different approaches than the self-report measurement approaches used in sport and exercise psychology. Emotion clearly is conceptualized as multidimensional, and the dimensions extend to physiological and evaluative dimensions as well as cognitive judgments.

CURRENT MEASUREMENT ISSUES IN SPORT AND EXERCISE PSYCHOLOGY

Although we have made progress, sport and exercise psychologists continue to debate issues related to individual-difference measures.

Proliferation

There are too many sport psychology measures. In the first edition of *Directory of Psychological Tests in the Sport and Exercise Sciences,* Ostrow (1990) listed almost 200 different measures. The updated edition now in preparation might well double that number. Very few of those measures meet even minimal psychometric standards of test development; most were simply developed and used for a particular study without preliminary item analyses and reliability and validity testing.

Statistical Shortcomings

As Schutz and Gessaroli (1993) noted, even when some psychometric information is provided, statistical methods are weak, often involving misapplication, misunderstanding, or misinterpretation of some aspect of factor analysis. Developers of sport psychology measures seldom use multitrait–mulitmethod matrices, typically ignore (if even acknowledge) conceptual models by using exploratory methods rather than confirmatory analyses, and often combine subscores (developed from analyses yielding uncorrelated factors) into global scores without ever checking for second-order factors or hierarchical structures.

Lack of Conceptual Clarity

To these statistical shortcomings identified by Schutz and Gessaroli (1993) I would add that sport psychologists usually stop psychometric analyses with alpha coefficients of internal consistency and never consider the more important validity issues. If measures are to be useful to sport and exercise psychology, they must validly measure some construct that is relevant to sport and exercise behavior. Of course, we cannot assess validity if we do not know what we are trying to measure, and we return to the bottom-line message: Conceptual clarity is the first step. If we know what we want to measure, we can consider validity of purported measures. Otherwise, inventories might include interrelated items yielding a score, but we have no justification for interpreting the score.

Even with the measures that were developed following appropriate psychometric standards, sport psychology has unresolved issues. Gauvin and Russell (1993) highlighted two key issues concerning our psychological measures—specificity and cross-cultural applications.

Specificity

The SCAT initiated the evolution to more sport-specific tests, sport psychology continued to move in that direction, and now we are at the point of deciding whether we have gone too far in that direction. For example, sport psychologists have developed measures of psychological skills (e.g., attentional style, sport confidence) specific to sport, but some sport psychologists advocate even more specificity. Measures of attentional style have been developed specific to tennis and to baseball/softball. The growing number of sport psychology consultants interested in assessing psychological skills of athletes for applied psychological skill training has added to this problem. A consulting or clinical perspective calls for very context-specific assessment for very specific purposes, and that might be at odds with the desire for more reliable and valid measures of psychological constructs. Sport-specific measures have advanced sport and exercise psychology research and practice, but further specificity detracts from generalizability and results in a case or clinical report that is not applicable or interpretable beyond the immediate situation.

Cross-Cultural Applications

Gauvin and Russell's (1993) second point relates to the cross-cultural use of psychological measures. This is a critical issue, as sport and exercise psychology is finally engaging in long-overdue cross-cultural and international research. Several measures have been translated and used around the world. For example, several PhD students working with me and with other advisors have used some of our anxiety and motivational measures in other countries. Translation of items and measures requires care. Some guidelines for translation, back-translation, and other procedures exist, but, beyond that, as Gauvin and Russell noted, we must also consider the cultural influences on the measures. Words, phrases, test items, and underlying constructs are related to their cultural context; when measures developed within one culture are taken to another, we might not be measuring the same thing.

Gauvin and Russell (1993) specifically discussed cross-cultural measures, but we can extend that issue to diversity in general. As sport and exercise psychology extends to more diverse physical activity contexts, we are dealing with more diverse participants, and our current measures typically developed for competitive sport participants in school settings might not be appropriate.

Developmental Issues

Developmental issues are a major concern as we examine different age groups. Measures for children are problematic and must consider developmental level, which involves not only language, cognitive, and attentional development but also the developmental meaning and understanding of constructs we are trying to assess. Developmental issues must also be considered with older adults. Like many colleagues, I am working with older adults in my recent research, and that brings up a variety of measurement issues. As well as attending to details such as large print and a limited number of items, the constructs and meanings are critical. Task and ego achievement orientation, which were prominent in my earlier research and remain prominent in current sport psychology research, are not large issues or even little issues for the older adults in my current research. Constructs that are of more concern (e.g., psychological well-being, efficacy for physical activity) take on different meanings for older adults and, moreover, vary greatly within the range of older adults.

Issues With Motivational Orientation Measures

In addition to the issues raised by Schutz and Gessaroli (1993) and Gauvin and Russell (1993), the motivational measures that dominate current sport and exercise psychology literature illustrate more specific measurement issues. Marsh (1994) examined some of sport psychology's more psychometrically sound measures of sport motivation orientation, including Roberts's (1993) Perceptions of Success Questionnaire (POS) and Gill and Deeter's (1988) SOQ. These measures are based on current social-cognitive achievement models emphasizing two general contrasting dispositional goal orientations variously termed (a) *mastery, task,* and *intrinsic orientation* and (b) *ego, competitive,* and *extrinsic orientation.* With his considerable psychometric skills and experience with such measures, Marsh compared the

POS and the SOQ and, based on varying correlations and confirmatory analyses, concluded that SOQ competitiveness reflects a task orientation, whereas POS competitiveness reflects an ego orientation.

Based on these findings and other observations of related measures, Marsh (1994) cautioned sport psychologists to beware of *jingle fallacies* (scales with the same label reflect the same construct) and *jangle fallacies* (scales with different labels measure different constructs) and to pursue construct-validity studies more vigorously to test the interpretations of measures. Marsh advocated validity studies, but we can also return to the bottom-line message: Conceptual clarity is the first step in specifying and delineating our constructs for later validation and interpretation.

Marsh's (1994) article suggests other issues. These goal-orientation measures are some of our most sound and widely used measures, but do we need them? Do they all measure unique, important constructs? Do the scales on the Task and Ego Orientation in Sport Questionnaire (TEOSQ; Duda, 1992), the POS, the SOQ, and other measures really reflect different underlying constructs, or are they all variations on a theme? Sport and exercise psychology specialists should ask these questions, as our students and colleagues continue to use these measures in research. Sport psychologists seem to be quick to use the measures but pay little attention to clarifying the questions and issues that prompted the development of such measures in the first place.

The availablity of these measures prompts sport psychologists to focus on the *P* part of the Lewin model to the neglect of other components, processes, and a holistic approach. For example, the TEOSQ has prompted us to rely on individual differences and dispositions in our research on goal-oriented behavior, but most theories and observations suggest that the immediate situation and larger social context have more influence on goal-directed behavior.

Even if dispositional measures such as the TEOSQ are appropriate, scoring and analysis are problematic. The TEOSQ, like many of the more widely used measures, is multidimensional, with task and ego subscales. Theoretical models suggest that high–task-oriented people behave in certain ways (e.g., persist in the face of challenges), whereas ego-oriented people behave differently (e.g., focus on outcomes, make comparisons to others). How are TEOSQ scores used to examine predictions? Some researchers use median splits to identify high-task and high-ego individuals, some look at difference scores, some use a 2 × 2 model, and still others use regression models with the range of scores. None matches the theory and measures very well. Personally, I don't like any of the solutions, but I use regression analyses because scores are distributed and clustered rather than extreme. However, scores are highly skewed (task scores are particularly high), regressions do not deal well with interactions or some of the theoretical predictions, and, again, sport psychologists have been distracted by the scoring and classification debates and have not attended to issues related to sport and exercise behavior.

Exercise/Physical Activity and Psychological Measures

Most of our better measures were developed for competitive sport contexts and do not tap constructs of more concern in the growing research related to exercise and health-related physical activity. Some motivational measures have been adapted for exercise settings, but the expanded research in this area requires more diverse measures. In particular, health-related quality of life (QOL; see Rejeski, Brawley, & Shumaker, 1996, for a review) is a construct with which many sport and exercise psychologists are struggling. National Institutes of Health funding guidelines call for the inclusion of QOL measures along with typical health and medical outcome measures, and QOL or psychological well-being is a practical concern for our content area. However, close inspection of the current QOL literature reveals a hodgepodge of varying combinations of selected depression, anxiety, and mood measures. So far, health psychologists and behavioral medicine researchers have provided little guidance in delineating coherent constructs and developing sound measures of health-related QOL. Sport and exercise psychologists, along with measurement colleagues, could contribute to this effort and further advance research and practice related to health-related physical activity.

STATISTICS AND DESIGN ISSUES

In this article, I purposely focus on the psychological measurement issues, because they are the most unique to the sport and exercise psychology area, and because they are indeed major issues. Sport and exercise psychology also has issues related to statistics and design. I do not address these issues in depth here. Other sources have covered statistical and design issues more effectively, and many of the issues are shared with other content areas and are covered in other articles in this issue of *Measurement in Physical Education and Exercise Science*. In this article, I highlight issues that are particularly relevant for sport and exercise psychology, noting progress and continuing issues.

At the 1993 conference of the International Society of Sport Psychology (ISSP), Schutz (1993) provided the following list of statistical and measurement issues in sport psychology:

- Hypothesis testing v. heuristic research
- When the null hypothesis is the research hypothesis
- The measurement and analysis of change
- Measuring the magnitude of an effect
- Statistical sophistication v. multivariate obfuscation
- The measurement of latent constructs
- The proliferation of scales and inventories
- Establishing the validity, reliability and stability of factor structures. (p. 119)

The last three issues relate to sport psychology measures and were covered in earlier sections. The first issue is significant for sport and exercise psychology but in a larger sense than was discussed by Schutz.

Qualitative Research Standards

For sport and exercise psychology, the issue is not really hypothesis testing *versus* heuristic research. Theoretical research can and should have heuristic value; as stated in Lewin's (1951) classic line, "there is nothing so practical as a good theory" (p. 169). The larger issue for sport and exercise psychology is dealing with the growing interest in "qualitative" research. Martens (1987) called for more heuristic research and adoption of alternative methods, such as case studies and introspective reports. Since then, several sport and exercise psychologists have incorporated alternative, qualitative methods, and some have provided models for that work. Scanlan, Stein, and Ravizza's (1989) work on sport enjoyment and stress, based on in-depth interviews with elite figure skaters, provided such a model.

Unfortunately, others have taken Martens's (1987) call for alternative approaches as justification for abandoning all scientific rigor, measurement standards, hypotheses testing, and statistical analyses. The best qualitative research, from my perspective, is done by scholars with experience in traditional methods who see new possibilities but not a cure-all, and who recognize limits of qualitative approaches and what they trade off by leaving traditional approaches. Good qualitative research—and it should be noted that qualitative research encompasses many diverse methods and approaches (see Denzin & Lincoln's excellent 1994 *Handbook on Qualitative Research*)—demands careful planning and rigor. The challenge for sport and exercise psychology, as well as for pedagogy and other content areas that incorporate qualitative approaches, is to develop standards and guidelines for conducting and evaluating that research. Content specialists are struggling with these issues, and any help from measurement specialists would be appreciated.

Statistical Issues

The null hypothesis as a research hypothesis is nonsensical, and I have no other insights to add beyond Schutz's (1993). However, I add that sport psychology research seldom presents clear, testable hypotheses, even when introductions appear to hypothesize something. Many sport and exercise psychology papers present results that "support" a model or theory, but careful reading of the introduction and consideration of the method reveal no way that any alternative results would have disproved the theory or led to any other conclusions. Clearly, sport and exercise psychology research is no model of Platt's (1964) "strong inference" approach, which Landers (1983) advocated for our area. Again, the point comes back to the bottom-line: Conceptual clarity is the first step.

Measurement of change is less central to our research now than it was 15 years ago when sport psychologists conducted more lab research with repeated trials of motor tasks. Related issues are more central for motor behavior, and is discussed in the Christina article in this issue.

Researchers are more inclined to measure the magnitude of effects and to report effect sizes and R^2 values in exercise and sport science publications. As Schutz (1993) pointed out, we still have far to go, and, moreover, sport psychologists can do much better evaluating the effects. This relates to a point Rejeski (1996) made in an American College of Sports Medicine (ACSM) lecture concerning QOL measures. Recently, Rejeski has been exploring physical activity and QOL with colleagues from medicine and health. In the ACSM lecture, he stated that ecological validity and clinical significance might well be more important than our typical psychometric tests regarding such issues. Researchers must develop measures of constructs and behaviors that are important to the health and well-being of our participants.

The issue of statistical sophistication versus multivariate obfuscation is my personal favorite. Many sport and exercise psychology papers offer multivariate obfuscation, often in misguided attempts to follow the advice of measurement and statistics specialists by using the most complex techniques and computer programs. Give us a hammer, and everything looks like a nail. More specifically, for sport and exercise psychology, it is an SPSS or LISREL program that hammers all data. About 10 years ago, MANOVA programs became commonplace, and many sport and exercise psychology reviewers and advisors told everyone to use MANOVA whenever possible. Today, I see similar enforcement of structural equation modeling (SEM) as the gateway to acceptability. Rather than view a multivariate method as the automatic solution, researchers should first ask if they have a multivariate question. If not, a multivariate method is not needed and probably not desirable. Correcting for experimentwise error rates with Bonferroni or other techniques might be a better alternative if the questions of interest involve separate univariate comparisons. Moreover, with multivariate results, scholars must be prepared for a complex and unclear multivariate interpretation. Statistical follow-up procedures are not universal, and the multivariate solutions do not fit our conceptual models very well.

SEM offers promise for sport and exercise psychology, and confirmatory factor analysis (CFA) certainly is appropriate to test or confirm a model. However, SEM is no substitute for careful and appropriate conceptualization and design. Many sport and exercise psychologists overinterpret SEM to infer causality and conceptual relations and forget that it is a statistical technique. Although CFA is appropriate to test a model, exploratory techniques might be more appropriate to delineate constructs and refine models. For example, multidimensional scaling (MDS) techniques are seldom used in sport and exercise psychology, but MDS might be a particularly promising approach for delineating and refining our constructs, models, and measures. Most of all, SEM, as well as any other statistical technique that dominates our research literature, tends to limit research. We plan and design studies that fit the techniques and measures rather than look first at our questions. Measurement specialists who are asked for statistical advice would do well to refuse to give any directions until content specialists specify a clear destination and question. Conceptual clarity is the first step to efficient research efforts and more useful research outcomes.

SUMMARY AND DIRECTIONS

We have made progress in sport and exercise psychology measurement and methodology, but few issues are resolved. Most of our progress and unresolved issues involve measures of our psychological constructs. Sport psychologists have developed sport-specific multidimensional measures and used them in conceptually based multivariate designs. Several unresolved issues relate to the psychometric properties of our measures and the appropriateness of our designs and analyses. However, the key issue, underlying all others, is the need for conceptual clarity. Sport and exercise psychologists must focus on the sport and exercise behaviors of interest, use appropriate conceptual models, and ask clear, relevant questions. Then we can work with measurement colleagues to find measures and methods that match those questions.

Further complicating the issues is the fact that sport and exercise psychology questions are changing. Not only must we clarify the current questions and models, but we must also prepare for new approaches. Specifically, the Lewin model, which still dominates sport and exercise psychology, is no longer sufficient. The Lewin model is linear and unidirectional, whereas current thought emphasizes dynamic processes and reciprocal relations and approaches the complexity notions that are taking over in other scientific areas. We must put the Lewin model into motion despite the realization that so doing will complicate the measurement and methodology issues beyond what can reasonably be addressed today.

For example, Bandura's (1977) original self-efficacy theory was a linear model with self-efficacy as the key mediating variable between interventions and behavior change. In his more recent social-cognitive framework, Bandura (1986) proposed a triadic, reciprocal relation among person (P), environment (E), and behavior (B), with the three constantly interacting with one another and changing over time. Similarly, Markus and Wurf (1987) proposed a dynamic self-concept that involves multiple interacting components constantly changing over time; Lazarus (1993) moved from his earlier conceptions of stress to a model of emotions that involves reciprocal, dynamic multidimensional relations.

Our current methods cannot deal adequately with these models. The best we can do is take snapshots when we need videotapes of the action. Measurement specialists cannot tell us how to measure, analyze, and interpret dynamic reciprocal relations and processes today. But, if sport and exercise psychologists set a clear destination, perhaps the measurement community can suggest steps in the right direction.

REFERENCES

Bandura, A. (1977). Self-efficacy: Toward a unifying theory of behavioral change. *Psychological Review, 84,* 191–215.

Bandura, A. (1986). *Social foundations of thought and action: A social cognitive theory.* Englewood Cliffs, NJ: Prentice Hall.

Carroll, L. (1992). *Alice's adventures in wonderland and Through the looking glass.* New York: Dell. (*Alice's adventures in wonderland* originally published in 1865)

Carron, A. V., Widmeyer, W. N., & Brawley, L. R. (1985). The development of an instrument to assess cohesion in sport teams: The Group Environment Questionnaire. *Journal of Sport Psychology, 7,* 244–266.

Denzin, N. K., & Lincoln, Y. S. (1994). *Handbook of qualitative research.* Thousand Oaks, CA: Sage.

Duda, J. L. (1992). Motivation in sport settings: A goal perspective approach. In G. C. Roberts (Ed.), *Motivation in sport and exercise* (pp. 57–91). Champaign, IL: Human Kinetics.

Gauvin, L., & Russell, S. J. (1993). Sport-specific and culturally adapted measures in sport and exercise psychology research: Issues and strategies. In R. N. Singer, M. Murphey, & L. K. Tennant (Eds.), *Handbook of research on sport psychology* (pp. 891–900). New York: Macmillan.

Gill, D. L., & Deeter, T. E. (1988). Development of the Sport Orientation Questionnaire. *Research Quarterly for Exercise and Sport, 59,* 191–202.

Gould, D., & Pick, S. (1995). Sport psychology: The Griffith era, 1920–1940. *The Sport Psychologist, 9,* 391–405.

Heil, J., & Henschen, K. (1996). Assessment in sport and exercise psychology. In J. L. Van Raalte & B. W. Brewer (Eds.), *Exploring sport and exercise psychology* (pp. 229–255). Washington, DC: American Psychological Association.

Landers, D. M. (1983). Whatever happened to theory testing in sport psychology? *Journal of Sport Psychology, 5,* 135–151.

Lazarus, R. S. (1993). From psychological stress to the emotions: A history of changing outlooks. *Annual Review of Psychology, 44,* 1–21.

Lewin, K. (1935). *A dynamic theory of personality.* New York: McGraw-Hill.

Lewin, K. (1951). *Field theory in social science.* New York: Harper.

Markus, H., & Wurf, E. (1987). The dynamic self-concept: A social psychological perspective. *Annual Review of Psychology, 38,* 299–337.

Marsh, H. W. (1994). Sport motivation orientations: Beware of jingle–jangle fallacies. *Journal of Sport & Exercise Psychology, 16,* 365–380.

Martens, R. (1975). *Sport Competition Anxiety Test.* Champaign, IL: Human Kinetics.

Martens, R. (1987). Science, knowledge, and sport psychology. *The Sport Psychologist, 1,* 29–55.

Martens, R., Vealey, R. S., & Burton, D. (1990). *Competitive anxiety in sport.* Champaign, IL: Human Kinetics.

Ostrow, A. C. (Ed.). (1990). *Directory of psychological tests in the sport and exercise sciences.* Morgantown, WV: Fitness Information Technology.

Platt, J. R. (1964). Strong inference. *Science, 146*(3642), 347–352.

Rejeski, W. J. (1996, May). *Quality of life in the elderly: Application to physical activity.* Tutorial lecture given at the meeting of the American College of Sports Medicine, Cincinnati, OH.

Rejeski, W. J., Brawley, L. R., & Shumaker, S. A. (1996). Physical activity and health-related quality of life. In J. O. Holloszy (Ed.), *Exercise and sport sciences reviews* (Vol. 24, pp. 71–108). Baltimore: Williams & Wilkins.

Roberts, G. C. (1993). Motivation in sport: Understanding and enhancing the motivation and achievement of children. In R. N. Singer, M. Murphey, & L. K. Tennant (Eds.), *Handbook of research on sport psychology* (pp. 405–420). New York: Macmillan.

Scanlan, T. K., Stein, G. L., & Ravizza, K. (1989). An in-depth study of former elite figure skaters: Part 2. Sources of enjoyment. *Journal of Sport & Exercise Psychology, 11,* 65–83.

Schutz, R. W. (1993). Methodological issues and measurement problems in sport psychology. In S. Serpa, J. Alves, V. Ferreira, & A. Paulo-Brito (Eds.), *Proceedings of the 8th World Congress of Sport Psychology* (pp. 119–131). Lisbon, Portugal: International Society of Sport Psychology.

Schutz, R. W., & Gessaroli, M. E. (1993). Use, misuse, and disuse of psychometrics in sport psychology research. In R. N. Singer, M. Murphey, & L. K. Tennant (Eds.), *Handbook of research on sport psychology* (pp. 901–917). New York: Macmillan.

Smith, R. E., Smoll, F. L., & Schutz, R. W. (1990). Measurement and correlates of sport-specific cognitive and somatic trait anxiety: The Sport Anxiety Scale. *Anxiety Research, 2,* 263–280.

Tutko, T. A., Lyon, L. P., & Ogilvie, B. C. (1969). *Athletic Motivation Inventory.* San Jose, CA: Institute for the Study of Athletic Motivation.

MEASUREMENT IN PHYSICAL EDUCATION AND EXERCISE SCIENCE, *1*(1), 55–69

Experimental and Statistical Design Issues in Human Movement Research

C. Roger James

Department of Health, Physical Education, and Recreation
Texas Tech University

Barry T. Bates

Department of Exercise and Movement Science
University of Oregon

Numerous research strategies exist for studying human behavior, including movement. Many experimental designs and statistical techniques are available, and the best technique to use in a given circumstance is a decision that must be made by the researcher (Bass, 1987). Most traditional designs (e.g., aggregate parametric linear models like *t* test, analysis of variance, and multiple analysis of variance) used today have flourished in the social and psychological sciences for the purpose of trying to understand human behavior.

R. A. Fisher, an agronomist and mathematician, developed the bases for most of the sophisticated group statistical procedures used today (Barlow & Hersen, 1984). However, it must be remembered that the root of these techniques was not the study of behavior but the study of average crop yield for a given plot of land (Barlow & Hersen, 1984; Fisher, 1925). Building on the philosophy, originated by Adolphe Quételet, that the average individual is the ideal goal rather than a statistical consequence, Fisher (1925) developed the properties for statistical tests that allowed for the generalization of results from a sample to the population (Barlow & Hersen, 1984). Questions regarding crop yield were not concerned with the health of individual plants but with total productivity of the plot (Barlow & Hersen, 1984; Payton, 1994).

Requests for reprints should be sent to C. Roger James, Department of Health, Physical Education, and Recreation, Box 43011, Texas Tech University, Lubbock, TX 79409–3011. E-mail: uncrj@ttacs.ttu.edu.

Philosophically, questions concerned with group behavior are very different from questions pertaining to the behavior or health of individuals, and yet the study of individuals has typically been discouraged by mainstream researchers. Interestingly, before Quételet and Fisher, most early physiological and behavioral research began with the intensive study of individual organisms by individuals such as Johannes Müller and Claude Bernard in the 1830s, Paul Broca in the 1860s, and I. P. Pavlov in the 1920s (Barlow & Hersen, 1984). Skinner (1966) noted that meaningful information was more likely to be obtained from studying just 1 rat for 1,000 hr than by studying 1,000 rats for 1 hr each (Bates, 1996; Skinner, 1966).

The popularity of group analysis techniques, as developed by Fisher, abounded during the 20th century because of the desire to generalize results, control experimental error, and apply scientific findings to real-life situations (particularly in applied settings). Group research designs were presumed to provide the generality of findings from a sample to the population and eventually allow conclusions about the individuals making up the population. Even today, many experts believe that the study of individual organisms limits the generality and thus the validity of results. In subsequent sections of this article, we discuss several of these misconceptions concerning the generality of both group and single-subject (SS) research designs.

Although most contemporary researchers believe strongly in the group-design approach, a review of the recent history (1960s to 1990s) of experimental design has revealed a resurgence in the philosophy and use of the individual as the basic unit of analysis, especially when the research questions deal with the behavior or health of the single individual (Bates, 1996; Bergin & Strupp, 1970; Bouffard, 1993; Conners & Wells, 1982; Edgington, 1987; Kratochwill, 1992; Sidman, 1960). SS experiments have a long tradition in behavioral medicine, and interest has emerged more recently in clinical medicine (Johannessen, Fosstvedt, & Petersen, 1991). Additionally, SS designs play a major role in many forms of applied and clinical research in behavioral and cognitive psychology, education, motor learning and control, adapted physical education, biomechanics, and other areas of study involving a large amount of subject heterogeneity (Bates, 1996; Bouffard, 1993; Kratochwill, 1992).

In human movement research, the primary goals should be to understand how individuals produce, manipulate, and respond to the internal and external factors involved in motion. Behavior (e.g., movement patterns, movement outcomes, performance) and health (e.g., injury prevention, treatment, rehabilitation) of the individual should be the primary focuses. No two individuals perform a task in an identical manner, and a given individual is unable to duplicate a previous performance due to the existence of variability (heterogeneity), which is inherent to movement both between and within individuals (James, 1996; Newel & Corcos, 1993). Therefore, it is asserted that the study of the individual should provide the primary thrust in human movement research.

HUMAN MOVEMENT CHARACTERISTICS

Human movement involves several important characteristics that must be considered when choosing a research design. Individually, these characteristics are not exclusive to human movement, but, in combination, they provide a novel complexity that makes meaningful research in this area particularly challenging.

The movements possible by humans are defined by at least three types of constraints—biomechanical, morphological, and environmental (Bernstein, 1967; Higgins, 1977). These constraints determine the types and magnitudes of motions possible within the neuromusculoskeletal system and delineate our movement potential from other animals and from other humans. *Biomechanical constraints* are limitations governed by physical laws that interact with a movement (Higgins, 1977). The individual must accommodate to factors such as gravity and friction and learn to manipulate the physical body within the boundaries that they provide. *Morphological constraints* are limitations imposed upon movement by the anatomical structure and functional capability of the individual. Variations in structure translate directly to diversity in movement patterns because of functional alterations in the ability to generate and manipulate force. *Environmental constraints* are movement limitations caused by the "spatial and temporal configuration of the world external to the organism" (Higgins, 1977, p. 45). Individuals interact with the environment continuously, and variations in the environment are reflected by variations in the movement sequence. Biomechanical, morphological, and environmental constraints do not act independently but interact on many different levels and in combination with previous experiences to determine the individual's expectations and movement potential.

When selecting a research design, human movement researchers must consider the appropriate level of analysis and level of movement organization that is the critical element of study. In an evolutionary sense, there are no variations in human traits; we are more alike than different. Typically, humans have two eyes, two legs, one heart, and similar neuromusculoskeletal anatomy and physiology (Bates, 1996; Bouffard, 1993). Because of these similarities, humans perform movements in essentially the same way. Movement capability is determined by the combined structures of our neuromuscular and musculoskeletal systems, which are broadly similar among individuals. Our neuromusculoskeletal system, generally similar but individually distinctive, provides a large but fixed number of options (degrees of freedom) for completing any given movement task. The system is functionally pliable in that changes (e.g., volition, perception, learning, growth and development) are possible within the bounds of the imposed movement constraints. Our musculoskeletal system is the least pliable component, as each individual's anatomic structure is largely dictated by heredity (e.g., joint structure, muscle fiber pennation characteristics, tendon insertion angle and location), although long-term variance from normal function can result in structural adaptations. Biomechanically, the distinctive differences among individuals provide numerous options for controlling the musculoskeletal system and result in a seemingly infinite number of functional degrees of freedom (movement options) within the system (Bates, 1996).

Variability is inherent within and between all biological systems (Newell & Corcos, 1993) and is the result of interactions among structural and functional characteristics of the neuromusculoskeletal system and the previously described constraints. Differences in movement potential due to the large number of available solutions within our systems provide individuals with an opportunity to perform movements utilizing different movement options or strategies. A movement strategy is a selected neuromusculoskeletal solution for the performance of a motor task. Strategy selection can be voluntary or involuntary, but its implementation results in a movement pattern unique to that individual at that moment in time within a specific environment. The availability of different strategies can result in a substantial amount of variability between individuals. Additionally, the selection of variant strategies by the same individual at different times will result in variability even when performing the same task.

An example of a movement strategy was described by Caster and Bates (1995) for the activity of landing on two feet after a short drop. In this experiment, the landing force upon impact experienced by each subject was measured both before and after the experimental manipulation of adding weight to a subject's ankles. Newtonian physics would predict that greater landing forces would be observed as more weight is added to the ankles. Although this was true for some subjects, others exhibited either no change or a decrease in landing force (Caster & Bates, 1995). These observations were explained by the existence of different subject strategies. A mechanical strategy resulted when the landing force increased proportionally to the magnitude of the external weight, and an accommodating strategy resulted when the landing force was disproportional, invariant, or inversely proportional to the additional weight. Response patterns can vary along a continuum from purely mechanical to fully accommodating (Bates, 1996), suggesting a wide variety of movement options available among different individuals and for the same individual at different times. Other studies have demonstrated the existence of strategies in a variety of circumstances (Dufek, Bates, Davis, & Malone, 1991; Jensen & Phillips, 1991; Lees & Bouracier, 1994; Schlaug, Knorr, & Seitz, 1994; Worringham, 1993).

When selecting a research design, researchers must consider these characteristics of human movement. Individuals are unique and should be recognized as the appropriate units of analysis when the research goal is to understand or affect behavior in areas such as high-level performance, injury, therapy, and learning (Bates, 1996).

RATIONALE FOR SS DESIGNS

An SS design is an experimental design in which one individual serves as the unit of study (i.e., $N = 1$ experiment). The behavior or performance of the subject is typically evaluated across time and under different treatment conditions, and the subject serves as his or her own control (Kazdin, 1982). SS designs provide a method for studying the behavior of a single individual when understanding that person's behavior is important or when large groups are not available for study (Bouffard, 1993; Johannessen, Fosstvedt, & Petersen, 1990; Payton, 1994). SS designs can also be used to study the behavior of individuals comprising a group when the application of a group design is inappropriate. Some researchers feel that SS designs might be more appropriate in the early stages of research because more information is made available to help generate new hypotheses or further assess existing theories (Bates, 1996; Johannessen et al., 1991; Payton, 1994).

SS designs are not advocated at the expense of group designs but are suggested as a supplement or an alternative when assumptions of the group design cannot be met. The appropriate experimental design in any circumstance is based on the research question and on the performance characteristics of the individuals being investigated (Bates, 1996). The goals of SS and group designs are identical, as both attempt to establish functional relations between independent and dependent variables while controlling or eliminating extraneous factors (Conners & Wells, 1982). In the following sections, we consider some of the criticisms of SS designs and discuss three issues critical to the rationale behind them—variability, aggregation, and generalization.

Variability

The amount of variability between individuals is (or should be) a major concern when selecting a research design to study human movement. The number of movement options available to any one individual and the inherent structural and functional differences between individuals create several different solutions for performing a given motor task. Typically, group designs either ignore or attempt to eliminate interindividual variability by the appropriate selection of experimental methodology (Barlow & Hersen, 1984; Bouffard, 1993; Bryk & Raudenbush, 1988). Group designs approach interindividual variability as error or nuisance to be controlled, so that the homogeneity-of-variance assumption is not violated (Barlow & Hersen, 1984; Bryk & Raudenbush, 1988). However, it has been shown repeatedly that individual subjects within a group often respond differentially to a treatment (Bates, 1996; Bouffard, 1993; Caster & Bates, 1995; Dufek et al., 1991; Johannessen et al., 1991). These differential responses are often unique and are not simply variations of the same movement solution or subject response. In the presence of differential responses, averaging or aggregating data across subjects can lead to the conclusion of "no significant effect" even though the effect might be substantial for individuals who respond positively or negatively to the treatment.

In the human movement domain, differential responses to the same treatment are called *strategies*. When subjects respond to a treatment utilizing different strategies, the homogeneity assumption is violated, as mixed responses define heterogeneity. When subjects exhibit heterogeneity, alternative approaches to traditional group aggregate designs must be considered. The SS approach is one alternative, and the presence of interindividual variability is the justification for this selection (Bates, 1996). Failure to account for individual subject strategies by assuming homogeneity can mask important information about subject behavior, promote misleading or incorrect conclusions about group or treatment effects, and reduce the possibility of detecting real differences by reducing statistical power (Bates, 1996; Bouffard, 1993; Bryk & Raudenbush, 1988; Johannessen & Fosstvedt, 1991). Barlow and Hersen (1984) emphasized that the more researchers understand about interindividual variability to a treatment, the easier it is to determine the effectiveness of that treatment for other individuals (i.e., generalizability).

In addition to accounting for heterogeneity by studying subjects individually, the SS approach can also serve as a preliminary evaluation tool for placing subjects into homogeneous groups before performing a group test. Conceptually, this approach consists of categorizing subjects by their preferred movement strategies, which preserves the homogeneity assumption of group statistical tests and reduces the potential for differential subject responses. Therefore, performing an SS analysis before the more traditional group approach is one method of ensuring relatively homogenous subject samples.

Aggregation

Many investigators, particularly those working in applied areas, have become increasingly dissatisfied with the traditional group approach (Barlow & Hersen, 1984). Complaints have arisen because of the weak association between experimental results and substantive issues limiting one's ability to predict or treat individual behavior (Barlow & Hersen, 1984; Bergin & Strupp, 1970). For example, the results of a group analysis indicated that psychotherapy made no difference to the mental health of patients when in fact the individual data revealed that some patients improved and others worsened, indicating a "cancellation" effect when the data were aggregated (Payton, 1994). The same result is common in human movement research when subjects utilizing different performance strategies are aggregated (Bates, 1996; Dufek, Bates, Stergiou, & James, 1995). The outcome of aggregation is a cancellation effect resulting in false support for the null hypothesis and a loss of information and interest in the research question.

Traditional statistical techniques use the group design in order to examine differences among different classes of data (i.e., subject groups or treatment conditions; Bouffard, 1993). The class mean (aggregate) is used to represent the performance of the entire class, and conclusions are drawn based on differences between the averages and are presumed to be true for each and every member of the class (Bouffard, 1993). Bakan (1955) emphasized the error in failing to distinguish between two types of propositions central to the ability to generalize results—general-type and aggregate-type propositions. A *general-type proposition* "asserts something which is presumably true of each and every member of a designable class"; an *aggregate-type proposition* "asserts something which is presumably true of the class considered as an aggregate" (Bakan, 1955, p. 211).

As the aim of science is to develop general principles or laws, the two types of propositions can therefore be viewed as the bases for making "lawful relationships about averages" (aggregate-type propositions) and "lawful relationships about people" (general-type propositions; Bouffard, 1993; p. 372). Taylor (1958) stated that, in order for a law to be universal, it must produce or predict the same (or similar) result in every person. Therefore, when the behavior of one or more individuals is of interest, experimental methodology such as SS designs utilizing general-type propositions should be incorporated.

Although the differences in aggregate and individual data have been acknowledged, it has been customary in group research to assume that the functional (mathematical) form of a mean data curve reflects the form of the individual curves (Estes, 1956). The rationale behind the previous arguments about individual versus aggregate data lies in the mathematical relations among the functions representing individual behavior. Several authors have demonstrated that individual subject data (e.g., hypothetical mathematical functions, functions representing subject behavior, learning curves), when averaged, can produce an aggregate curve unlike any of the individual component curves (Baloff & Becker, 1967; Bouffard, 1993; Estes, 1956). The explanation is that differential effects cancel one another out when averaged (Baloff & Becker, 1967), whereas similar components can be accentuated. Consequently, use of aggregate data to predict individual behavior might yield little or no information about individuals or might completely misrepresent the types of individual behavior from which the aggregate arose (Baloff & Becker, 1967; Bouffard, 1993; Estes, 1956). Therefore, inductive inference from the mean to the individual is impossible (Estes, 1956).

In human movement research, differences between information obtained from individuals and information obtained from aggregate data were demonstrated in two different studies (Bates & Stergiou, 1996; Dufek et al., 1995). Both studies performed group and SS analyses on their respective subject-variable data sets in order to determine how the choice of an analysis technique might influence experimental conclusions. Although different group techniques were used in these studies, both sets of researchers concluded that the group results were not representative of the individual subject results.

Generalization

One major criticism of SS designs is the apparent inability to generalize results from a sample to the population (Bates, 1996). However, based on the potential problems of aggregating data over a heterogeneous group, a similar claim can be made about group designs. Generalization of results are limited to units of the same level included in the experiment. Barlow and Hersen (1984) wrote that SS designs actually produce greater generality than group designs because they account for interindividual variability rather than averaging it out. One method for improving the generality of group designs is to make groups as homogeneous as possible (Barlow & Hersen, 1984; Bates, 1996). The limitation of this approach, at least for one-time-only studies, is that the generalizations are confined only to groups that are homogeneous on the same relevant characteristics. The obvious solution to generalizing beyond a narrowly defined group or a single individual is replication (Barlow & Hersen, 1984).

Most researchers believe that a large sample size is better than a small sample size for generalizing results to the population (Bouffard, 1993; Kazdin, 1982). Although this is one argument against SS designs, generality is based on the number of particulars (i.e., replications) and not on the sample size (Bass, 1987). The more times an effect can be demonstrated within different samples, the greater the likelihood the effect will occur within the population (Bates, 1996). Group designs, regardless of sample size, test the theory only once for each experiment conducted, but SS designs test the theory each time a subject is evaluated (Bakan, 1955; Bouffard, 1993; Valsiner, 1986). Modifications or refinements to the theory can be made by evaluating additional individuals (Bates, 1996). In this way, several response types (i.e., strategies) might be identified, thus permitting the grouping of like responders and the possible formulation or modification of a general principle. Using this approach, as one might do when exploring new research hypotheses, it would be beneficial to select subjects who exhibit a broad spectrum of movement strategies (i.e., a heterogeneous group), thereby allowing representation of movement patterns from all along the previously described performance continuum.

Several researchers have described two basic types of replication relating to the generality of results—direct and systematic (Bass, 1987; Mace & Kratochwill, 1986; Sidman, 1960). *Direct replication* is the exact repetition of an experiment with the same or different subjects (Bass, 1987; Mace & Kratochwill, 1986; Sidman, 1960), which allows generalization to other individuals; *systematic replication* is repetition of an experiment across a variety of similar (but not identical) situations (Bass, 1987; Mace & Kratochwill, 1986; Sidman, 1960), which allows generalization across situations, variables, and subjects. Both types of replication allow researchers to control threats to internal validity while providing a method for demonstrating generality (external validity; Bass, 1987; Mace & Kratochwill, 1986). Although both replication types are important, systematic replication is the primary method used by SS researchers to demonstrate generality of results (Bass, 1987).

How many SS replications are required to demonstrate a reasonable probability that a behavior occurs in the population? Denenberg (1982) claimed that only one or two cases beyond the original are needed to establish the existence of a trait in the population:

> It can be shown (Denenberg, 1978) that, if one draws a sample of fifty cases and if at least one case yields a finding that matches the original one, the probability that this occurred by chance alone is less than 0.05. If the sample has more than fifty cases but fewer than three hundred and fifty, then the probability value of finding two more cases [by chance] like the original is less than 0.05. (Denenberg, 1982, p. 30)

Therefore, to establish generality by replicating an SS experiment, only a relatively small sample size might be required.

A slightly more conservative but straightforward method of estimating probability is to perform a series of replicated SS experiments and evaluate the percentage of individuals demonstrating the characteristic of interest. If more than 5% of the subjects exhibit the trait, then the probability of that trait occurring in the sample due to some factor other than chance is greater than .05 (i.e., the probability of it occurring by chance alone is less than .05). However, if fewer than 5% of the individuals exhibit the characteristic, then it is likely that the trait was a chance result. This method of estimating probability requires that the experiment be replicated enough times to demonstrate reliable outcomes, and, the more individuals included, the greater the generality.

DATA-ANALYSIS ISSUES IN SS EXPERIMENTS

The preceding discussion attempted to justify the need for SS designs in human movement research. Although selecting the appropriate design is a critical step in the planning of an experiment, once the need for an SS design has been established, several data-analysis issues should be considered. It is beyond the scope of this article to detail all of the available design implementations within SS research, and so we direct the reader to Barlow and Hersen (1984) and Edgington (1987) for additional information. The purpose of this section is to outline two basic data-analysis options a researcher can consider when performing an SS analysis—nonparametric tests and parametric tests. Nonparametric tests typically require fewer assumptions and are often used when the parametric assumptions cannot be met; parametric tests are generally robust and are not seriously affected by moderate violations of their assumptions, thus permitting their use in a wide variety of circumstances (McCall, 1986). The selection of either a parametric or nonparametric test depends largely on the nature of the data and the information sought. With respect to SS analyses, both types of statistical techniques have been recommended (Bates, 1996; Busk & Marascuilo, 1992; Edgington, 1987; Huitema, 1985), but there is some controversy surrounding the appropriate use of parametric tests.

Parametric Tests

Traditional (parametric) statistical tests have been advocated for use in SS designs, given that the appropriate assumptions are satisfied (Bates, 1996; Huitema, 1985). The failure to meet these assumptions, which include normality and trial (response) independence, has brought criticisms from many group- and SS-design authorities including manuscript reviewers and journal editors (Edgington, 1987). Criticisms about the violation of assumptions have been addressed previously (Bates, 1996) and are briefly discussed here.

In human movement research, parametric tests conducted within an SS design are no more problematic with respect to violating assumptions than when performing the same tests within a group analysis. In an SS analysis, sample size is determined by the number of trials (responses) generated by the subject and not from the number of subjects. Statistical power and response reliability are gained by increasing the number of trials performed (Bates, Dufek, & Davis, 1992). Data normality is determined based on distribution of the dependent variable values for the trials performed during each treatment condition. Severe violations of normality could preclude the use of parametric tests, although Keppel (1982) explained that even the most extremely skewed data sets might affect probability levels only a maximum of 3 percentage points.

Bates (1996) investigated the normality of human movement data obtained during a series of experiments consisting of more than 500 individual subject-variable data sets. The distribution of values for one subset of dependent variables (16) exhibited statistical non-normality ($p > .05$) for 100% of the cases, suggesting support for the previously described criticism. However, these non-normal results were for dependent variables in close proximity to an absolute physical or temporal limit, thus allowing them to vary predominantly in only one direction and restricting the shape of the distribution. In contrast, variables influenced less by the absolute limits tended to exhibit normality (Bates, 1996) and were generally within the limits of tolerance for the robust parametric tests, as described by Keppel (1982).

Dufek et al. (1995) evaluated the normality of several variable data sets obtained during various running activities. Normality was tested using a curve correlation technique (Shapiro–Wilk procedure, W). The average W value across all subjects was .938, with the lowest value reported to be .910 for one subject (Dufek et al., 1995). These results suggested a high degree of similarity between the dependent variable and normal distributions.

Although some SS variable data sets vary with regard to normality, the physical and temporal constraints affecting the dependent variables are not unique to SS analyses. Careful researchers, whether advocates of SS or group designs, should be familiar with the distribution of variables commonly used in their areas of study. Further investigation is needed in order to determine the degrees of normality or non-normality for both aggregate and SS human movement variables.

Like the violation of the assumption of normality, the violation of the assumption of independence is another criticism against the use of parametric tests in SS experiments. The concern for independence (i.e., serial dependency or autocorrelation) in SS experiments pertains to the relations among trials rather than the relationships among subjects. Most researchers who oppose the use of parametric tests in SS analyses cite serial dependency as the major concern (Huitema, 1985; Johannessen et al., 1990). There are two primary problems with autocorrelated data: (a) Errors are not independent, and so statistical tests overestimate the number of independent sources of information; (b) by altering the error variance, positive and negative autocorrelations can create liberal and conservative biases, respectively (Busk & Marascuilo, 1992). Two opposing views about autocorrelation predominate among behavioral researchers. One view maintains that all behavioral measurements taken from one subject are correlated (Busk & Marascuilo, 1992); the other view holds that responses within a subject are independent as long as they do not have an effect on one another (Huitema, 1985). Huitema (1985) demonstrated among several behavioral data sets that serial dependency was not a factor. Evaluation of more than 500 previously identified subject-variable data sets (Bates, 1996) identified only 4.97% significant correlations at the $p < .05$ level, supporting trial independence.

In human movement research, Bates (1996; Bates et al., 1992) presented a model of human performance representing individual subjects (when examined in isolation) as normal-distribution random-trial generators. In this model, subjects were viewed to produce responses statistically independent both within and between treatment conditions (Bates, 1996). Subject responses were viewed as independent because of the inherent variability that occurs within the neuromuscular system when executing movements. Because the sources of variability are believed to originate from either random errors (Schmidt, Zelaznik, Hawkins, Frank, & Quinn, 1979) or chaotic fluctuations (Kelso & Ding, 1993) inherent within the neuromotor system, the variability in movement outcomes was modeled to reflect these variability sources. Experimental data supporting the model were presented by Bates (1996), and the model has been used in other studies (Bates et al., 1992; Dufek et al., 1995) to gain a better understanding of selected aspects of human performance. Therefore, when SS human movement data fit the presented model, independence of trials may be assumed, and thus parametric tests may be employed.

Nonparametric Tests

Severe violations of the statistical assumptions of normality and independence might preclude the use of parametric tests in favor of nonparametric tests. Several nonparametric techniques have been applied to behavioral data, including the Mann–Whitney U test, Fisher's exact test, the Wampold–Worsham test, the Marascuilo–Busk test, and randomization tests (Edgington, 1992). Few researchers (none familiar to the current authors) have applied nonparametric techniques to SS human movement data, although many nonparametric group tests are described in behavioral and biomedical science statistics texts (Huntsberger & Leaverton, 1970; McCall, 1986). As many researchers justify not using SS designs because of threats to statistical assumptions, nonparametric tests seem to provide a logical alternative. Randomization tests, in particular, have been recommended for use in behavioral and biomedical science SS experiments when random sampling is questionable or not possible (Edgington, 1987, 1992; Johannessen et al., 1991).

Randomization tests are nonparametric tests that are not dependent on the assumptions of random sampling of subject responses or specific data distributions (Edgington, 1992; Johannessen & Fosstvedt, 1991). Procedurally, a randomization test is performed by computing a test statistic (e.g., t, F) on the data as collected experimentally. The data are permuted in all possible ways (i.e., all possible combinations of trials assigned to conditions), and the test statistic is computed for each permutation. The significance of the randomization test (p value) is determined by the proportion of permutation test statistics that are greater than or equal to the one computed for the original data set (Edgington, 1987, 1992; Johannessen et al., 1990). For example, if 5% of the test statistics are greater than or equal to the original, then the randomization test p value is equal to .05. The more permutations computed, the smaller the p values that can be obtained (Johannessen et al., 1990). Randomization tests meet the requirements for a randomized design, even in the absence of random sampling (Edgington, 1992). The only assumption required in a randomization test is that the observed responses could have been obtained regardless of the arrangement of trials within or between experimental conditions (Johannessen et al., 1990). Edgington (1992) wrote, "The objective of a randomization test is to determine how rarely a test statistic value as extreme as the experimental value would result from random assignment alone, in the absence of a treatment effect" (p. 136). Randomization tests may provide an acceptable alternative to parametric tests when assumptions are violated, although further investigation is required to determine how reliably these data-analysis options represent SS human movement data.

RECOMMENDATIONS

The purpose of this article was to present and support the use of an alternative research approach in the study of human movement when subject heterogeneity contra-indicates use of a group design. Bass (1987) summarized the arguments in favor of SS designs:

1. Group data may not represent intra-individual processes.
2. Group and individual data answer different questions.

3. Identification of intersubject variability sources is crucial for extending the generality of a treatment.
4. Generality is a function of the number of particulars (i.e., replications) and not sample size.

Given the arguments and evidence presented in support of SS designs and the discussion surrounding the use of nonparametric and parametric tests, the following procedures are recommended:

1. Use SS designs to examine an individual's performance.
2. Use a series of similarly conducted SS experiments to support the generality of conclusions.
3. Combine SS and group analyses to gain a better understanding of the data.
4. Justify that dependent variables fit statistical assumptions before performing parametric tests.
5. Validate use of parametric tests by comparing their p values to those of randomization tests (Edgington, 1992; Johannessen et al., 1990).
6. Use randomization tests when parametric statistical assumptions are severely violated.

REFERENCES

Bakan, D. (1955). The general and the aggregate: A methodological distinction. *Perceptual and Motor Skills, 5,* 211–212.

Baloff, N., & Becker, S. W. (1967). On the futility of aggregating individual learning curves. *Psychological Reports, 20,* 183–191.

Barlow, D. H., & Hersen, M. (1984). *Single case experimental designs: Strategies for studying behavior change.* New York: Pergamon.

Bass, R. F. (1987). The generality, analysis, and assessment of single-subject data. *Psychology in the Schools, 24,* 97–104.

Bates, B. T. (1996). Single-subject methodology: An alternative approach. *Medicine and Science in Sports and Exercise, 28,* 631–638.

Bates, B. T., Dufek, J. S., & Davis, H. P. (1992). The effect of trial size on statistical power. *Medicine and Science in Sports and Exercise, 24,* 1059–1068.

Bates, B. T., & Stergiou, N. (1996). *Impact force accommodation strategies.* Manuscript submitted for publication.

Bergin, A. E., & Strupp, H. H. (1970). New directions in psychotherapy research. *Journal of Abnormal Psychology, 76,* 13–26.

Bernstein, N. (1967). *The co-ordination and regulation of movements.* Oxford, England: Pergamon.

Bouffard, M. (1993). The perils of averaging data in adapted physical activity research. *Adapted Physical Activity Quarterly, 10,* 371–391.

Bryk, A. S., & Raudenbush, S. W. (1988). Heterogeneity of variance in experimental studies: A challenge to conventional interpretations. *Psychological Bulletin, 3,* 396–404.

Busk, P. L., & Marascuilo, L. A. (1992). Statistical analysis in single-case research: Issues, procedures, and recommendations, with applications to multiple behaviors. In T. R. Kratochwill & J. R. Levin

(Eds.), *Single-case research design and analysis: New directions for psychology and education* (pp. 159–185). Hillsdale, NJ: Lawrence Erlbaum Associates, Inc.

Caster, B. L., & Bates, B. T. (1995). The assessment of mechanical and neuromuscular response strategies during landing. *Medicine and Science in Sports and Exercise, 27,* 736–744.

Conners, C. K., & Wells, K. C. (1982). Single-case designs in psychopharmacology. In A. E. Kazdin & A. H. Tuma (Eds.), *New directions for methodology of social and behavioral sciences: Single-case research designs* (Vol. 13, pp. 61–76). San Francisco: Jossey-Bass.

Denenberg, V. H. (1982). Comparative psychology and single-subject research. In A. E. Kazdin & A. H. Tuma (Eds.), *New directions for methodology of social and behavioral sciences: Single-case research designs* (Vol. 13, pp. 19–31). San Francisco: Jossey-Bass.

Dufek, J. S., Bates, B. T., Davis, H. P., & Malone, L. A. (1991). Dynamic performance assessment of selected sport shoes on impact forces. *Medicine and Science in Sports and Exercise, 23,* 1062–1067.

Dufek, J. S., Bates, B. T., Stergiou, N., & James, C. R. (1995). Interactive effects between group and single-subject response patterns. *Human Movement Science, 14,* 301–323.

Edgington, E. S. (1987). Randomized single-subject experiments and statistical tests. *Journal of Counseling Psychology, 34,* 437–442.

Edgington, E. S. (1992). Non-parametric tests for single case experiments. In T. R. Kratochwill & J. R. Levin (Eds.), *Single-case research design and analysis: New directions for psychology and education* (pp. 133–157). Hillsdale, NJ: Lawrence Erlbaum Associates, Inc.

Estes, W. K. (1956). The problem of inference from curves based on group data. *Psychological Bulletin, 53,* 134–140.

Fisher, R. A. (1925). On the mathematical foundations of the theory of statistics. In Cambridge Philosophical Society (Ed.), *Theory of statistical estimation: Proceedings of the Cambridge Philosophical Society* (pp. 700–725). England.

Higgins, J. R. (1977). *Human movement: An integrated approach.* St. Louis, MO: Mosby.

Huitema, B. E. (1985). Autocorrelation in applied behavior analysis: A myth. *Behavioral Assessment, 7,* 107–118.

Huntsberger, D. V., & Leaverton, P. E. (1970). *Statistical inference in the biomedical sciences.* Boston: Allyn & Bacon.

James, C. R. (1996). *Effects of overuse injury proneness and task difficulty on joint kinetic variability during landing.* Unpublished doctoral dissertation, University of Oregon, Eugene.

Jensen, J. L., & Phillips, S. J. (1991). Variations on the vertical jump: Individual adaptations to changing task demands. *Journal of Motor Behavior, 23,* 63–74.

Johannessen, T., & Fosstvedt, D. (1991). Statistical power in single subject trials. *Family Practice, 8,* 384–387.

Johannessen, T., Fosstvedt, D., & Petersen, H. (1990). Statistical aspects of controlled single subject trials. *Family Practice, 7,* 325–328.

Johannessen, T., Fosstvedt, D., & Petersen, H. (1991). Combined single subject trials. *Scandinavian Journal of Primary Health Care, 9,* 23–27.

Johnston, J. M. (1982). The role of individual data in laboratory investigations of operant conditioning. In A. E. Kazdin & A. H. Tuma (Eds.), *New directions for methodology of social and behavioral sciences: Single-case research designs* (Vol. 13, pp. 49–59). San Francisco: Jossey-Bass.

Kazdin, A. E. (1982). Single-case experimental designs in clinical research and practice. In A. E. Kazdin & A. H. Tuma (Eds.), *New directions for methodology of social and behavioral sciences: Single-case research designs* (Vol. 13, pp. 33–47). San Francisco: Jossey-Bass.

Kelso, J. A. S., & Ding, M. (1993). Fluctuations, intermittency, and controllable chaos in biological coordination. In K. M. Newell & D. M. Corcos (Eds.), *Variability and motor control* (pp. 291–316). Champaign, IL: Human Kinetics.

Keppel, G. (1982). *Design and analysis: A researcher's handbook.* Englewood Cliffs, NJ: Prentice Hall.

Kratochwill, T. R. (1992). Single-case research design and analysis: An overview. In T. R. Kratochwill & J. R. Levin (Eds.), *Single-case research design and analysis: New directions for psychology and education* (pp. 1–14). Hillsdale, NJ: Lawrence Erlbaum Associates, Inc.

Lees, A., & Bouracier, J. (1994). The longitudinal variability of ground reaction forces in experienced and inexperienced runners. *Ergonomics, 37,* 197–206.

Mace, F. C., & Kratochwill, T. R. (1986). The individual subject in behavior analysis research. In J. Valsiner (Ed.), *The individual subject and scientific psychology* (pp. 153–180). New York: Plenum.

McCall, R. B. (1986). *Fundamental statistics for behavioral sciences.* San Diego: Harcourt Brace Jovanovich.

Newell, K. M., & Corcos, D. M. (1993). Issues in variability and motor control. In K. M. Newell & D. M. Corcos (Eds.), *Variability and motor control* (pp. 1–12). Champaign, IL: Human Kinetics.

Payton, O. D. (1994). *Research: The validation of clinical practice.* Philadelphia: Davis.

Schlaug, G., Knorr, U., & Seitz, R. J. (1994). Inter-subject variability of cerebral activations in acquiring a motor skill: A study with position emission tomography. *Experimental Brain Research, 98,* 523–534.

Schmidt, R. A., Zelaznik, H., Hawkins, B., Frank, J. S., & Quinn, J. T. (1979). Motor-output variability: A theory for the accuracy of rapid motor acts. *Psychological Review, 86,* 415–452.

Sidman, M. (1960). *Tactics of scientific research: Evaluating experimental data in psychology.* New York: Basic.

Skinner, B. F. (1966). Operant behavior. In W. K. Honig (Ed.), *Operant behavior: Areas of research and application* (pp. 74–78). New York: Appleton–Century–Crofts.

Taylor, J. G. (1958). Experimental design: A cloak for intellectual sterility. *British Journal of Psychology, 49,* 106–116.

Valsiner, J. (1986). Different perspectives on individual-based generalizations in psychology. In J. Valsiner (Ed.), *The individual subject and scientific psychology* (pp. 391–404). New York: Plenum.

Worringham, C. J. (1993). Predicting motor performance from variability measures. In K. M. Newell & D. M. Corcos (Eds.), *Variability and motor control* (pp. 53–63). Champaign, IL: Human Kinetics.

MEASUREMENT IN PHYSICAL EDUCATION AND EXERCISE SCIENCE, *1*(1), 71–87

Using Old Research Ideas to Study Contemporary Problems in Adapted Physical Activity

Marcel Bouffard

Faculty of Physical Education and Recreation
University of Alberta

Concepts that have proved useful for ordering things easily assume so great an authority over us that we easily forget their terrestrial origin and accept them as unalterable facts. They then become labelled as "conceptual necessities," *"a priori* givens," etc. The road of scientific progress is frequently blocked for long periods by such errors. It is therefore not just an idle game to exercise our ability to analyze familiar concepts, and to demonstrate the conditions under which their justification and usefulness depend. (Einstein, 1916, cited in Holton, 1988, p. vi)

A major purpose of the 8th Measurement and Evaluation Symposium, *Exploring the Kaleidoscope* (October 24 to 26, 1996, Oregon State University, Corvallis), was to explore measurement, research design, and statistics issues in selected subdisciplines of exercise and sport science. I am glad to have this opportunity to represent the community of adapted physical activity researchers and present some of my ideas about research design, statistics, and measurement issues in this field. I must confess immediately that I have little to say about program evaluation. You should not infer from this that the adapted physical activity field does not have evaluation problems and issues. To the contrary, the evaluation of our services and programs to special populations has been neglected for many years. Instead, I present some old and possibly forgotten ideas. I think that these old ideas are useful and might help us to develop excellent research programs in adapted physical activity and possibly in the study of the psychology of sport and exercise.

Requests for reprints should be sent to Marcel Bouffard, Faculty of Physical Education and Recreation, University of Alberta, Edmonton, Alberta, T6G 2H9, Canada. E-mail: mbouffar@per. ualberta.ca.

During my doctoral program, I received traditional training in univariate and multivariate statistics. In the measurement area, I was exposed to classical true-score theory, generalizability theory, and basic concepts of item-response theory. I can easily remember the enthusiasm and the frustration I felt while taking these courses. I viewed them as a special key that could give me privileged access to knowledge about the world. In contrast, I was struggling with the possible application of ideas presented in class. In adapted physical education, the harsh reality was that the accessible population was usually very small and heterogeneous. I remember a graduate student colleague who wanted to complete his doctoral dissertation with deaf children with spina bifida. He could find only two children within the surrounding area (population = 750,000).

With hindsight, I realize that my thinking during my graduate years was guided primarily by pragmatic considerations and the graduate education culture in which I was embedded. After all, serious and well-respected scholars had been thinking about the problem of knowledge generation before me. During my doctoral education, I was exposed to the problem of induction as expressed by Hume (1740/1888). Hume asserted that it is impossible to infer a true statement about all members of a class on the basis of observing only some members of that class (Angeles, 1981). With this understanding, D. T. Campbell and Stanley (1963) and, later, T. D. Cook and D. T. Campbell (1979) produced an epistemology of knowledge in which you reduce the plausibility of rival hypotheses. Central to their thinking was that, to infer causality, you should control for confounding variables, randomize whenever possible, and study large groups of people. The message I received was that the generation of knowledge about special populations was made easier by studying large groups of (homogeneous) people. Stated differently, expert university professors were telling me in a kind but firm way that I could not study the small groups in which I was interested. I concluded that methodology was constraining research questions (although it was often denied in my professors' discourse), as my questions were largely about individuals who were "outliers."

My view about adapted physical activity research has changed substantially over the last 15 years. I have several questions to share about the appropriateness of traditional group-design research as well as the individual-difference approach (Cronbach, 1957, 1975). Moreover, I no longer see small and heterogeneous samples as a major obstacle to knowledge generation.

Here I do not elaborate on traditional research-design ideas as presented in textbooks like D. T. Campbell and Stanley's (1963), T. D. Cook and D. T. Campbell's (1979), Kirk's (1982), Maxwell and Delaney's (1990), and Winer's (1971). I assume that these fundamental ideas are well known by the exercise and sport science research community. Instead, I present ideas that have been mostly forgotten. I no longer assume that newer ideas are better than old ones. I have rejected the belief that researchers, as a group, are essentially rational people who can gradually converge on the best idea. Key ideas retained by a scientific community are often influenced by the socio-historico-political context at the time that they become accepted by a community of scientists (Danziger, 1990). It is impossible to demonstrate the truth of empirical statements. The best we can hope for is to show their plausibility.

The importance of studying the history of ideas is often lost in our discipline. Of particular importance is the evolution of three ideas—the evolution of the meaning of key words like *nomothetic* and *idiographic,* the historical development of research procedures in psychology, and the changes in perceptions and treatment of persons with a disability during the last 150 years. These ideas are discussed here to help you understand actual trends and forecast key questions and issues to be asked by the field during the third millennium. Although at first glance these ideas might appear to be unrelated, they are not. These thoughts are integrated to present a particular vision of research with human participants. These ideas are particularly important for the adapted physical activity field; however, their potential relevance to the psychology of sport and physical activity should gradually become clear.

To some, these thoughts may be provocative, even heretical. Yet, the expression and constructive criticism of differences in research assumptions are an essential part of the ongoing process of inquiry, reflection, and development in any field of research. These comments will generate more questions than answers. However, as experts in cognitive science would say, problem representation is a first and essential step to the problem-solving process. The groundwork for new approaches requires some appreciation of the limitations of past and current thinking.

NOMOTHETIC AND IDIOGRAPHIC KNOWLEDGE

The German philosopher Windelband (1904) is often credited with the introduction of the word *nomothetic* to refer to knowledge about "what always is" (Lamiell, 1995). This word is rooted in the Greek *nomos* plus *tketikos,* which means "lawful thesis" (Lamiell, 1987). To Windelband, nomothetic knowledge is what reappears across particular instances. Nomothetic research is the search for universal, abstract principles or laws. For example, had Windelband studied short-term memory and observed a U-shaped serial position curve for each participant in the study, he would have concluded, within the limits of induction (Hume, 1740/1888), that this knowledge is nomothetic. To become nomothetic knowledge, an empirical statement concerning some aspect of the psychological functioning of persons must be generalizable across persons (Lamiell, 1995). Evidence for similarity of findings "must be *repeatedly* uncovered in studies of *many* individual persons examined *one at a time*" (Lamiell, 1995, p. 160).

In contrast, the word *idiographic* is rooted in the Greek word *idios,* meaning "one's own, private" plus *tketikos* (Frank, 1986). Idiographic laws are regularities associated with an individual instead of a group, and the goal of this approach is to discover regularities at the individual level (instead of at the group level). For example, when asked by his mother what he did last night, an adolescent might constantly lie. Another example is the golfer who regularly makes better contact with the ball when she keeps her eyes on the ball until ball contact. To Windelband, idiographic studies are often an essential step in the generation of nomothetic knowledge. Each person's uniqueness is not viewed as an obstacle to generalization about universal psychological laws. According to Windelband, it is possible to have idiographic analyses followed by a nomothetic conclusion.

The conceptual distinctions originally made by Windelband have not been preserved in the literature pertaining to the nomothetic–idiographic controversy (Lamiell, 1991). The expressions *nomothetic* and *idiographic* knowledge now often refer to statements made following the use of particular research methods. Because their results are based on more than one person, traditional group-design methods (e.g., Kirk, 1982; Maxwell & Delaney, 1990; Winer, 1971) or between-subject correlational methods (e.g., Darlington, 1990; Mueller, 1996; Thorndike, 1978) are frequently viewed as nomothetic methods. According to this research perspective, nomothetic knowledge results from the study of aggregate values (e.g., mean, variance, correlation). In constrast, case-study methodology (e.g., Yin, 1989) and single-case research design (e.g., Barlow & Hersen, 1984; Kratochwill & Levin, 1992) are often viewed as exemplars of idiographic research because their results are often based on the intensive study of one person.

Although the purpose of science is still hotly debated in some milieus, it is frequently stated that the aim of science is the discovery of universal regularities (Kaplan, 1964). Science, it is often said, is the search for nomothetic laws. In contrast, single-subject designs have been associated with the discovery of the uninteresting and irrelevant particulars. Idiographic methods have been severely criticized by some researchers because idiographic knowledge is often associated with $N = 1$ methods. The late psychometrician Jum C. Nunnally (1978) wrote:

> The idiographists may be entirely correct, but if they are, it is a sad day for psychology. Idiography is an antiscience point of view: it discourages the search for general laws and instead encourages the description of particular phenomena (people). (p. 548)

The identification of nomothetic and idiographic knowledge with methods used to generate that knowledge has been frequently criticized (Allport, 1962; Lamiell, 1987; Valsiner, 1986a). I suggest here that the original conceptualization of the term *nomothetic* made by Windelband (1904, as cited by Lamiell, 1995) be reinstated. Contrary to Nunnally's (1978) viewpoint, my contention here is that true nomothetic knowledge, as defined by Windelband (1904), must start with an idiographic analysis. To be qualified as nomothetic knowledge, a psychological "law has to be valid for *each single* subject and not for an *average* subject" (Wottawa, 1990, p. 67). The aggregation of data across persons might not lead to the discovery of nomothetic knowledge as defined by Windelband.

OVERVIEW OF HISTORICAL DEVELOPMENT OF
RESEARCH IN PSYCHOLOGY

In his book on the historical development of research in psychology, Danziger (1990) identified three major methodological traditions—the Leipzig model, the clinical experiment model, and the Galton model. Only a brief survey of these traditions is made here.

Leipzig Research Model

This research orientation originated with Wilhelm Wundt at the University of Leipzig in 1879 (Danziger, 1987, 1990). Clearly, statistical methodology was used in this laboratory, as reflected in the use of Fechnerian psychophysics (Danziger, 1987). An essential characteristic of this methodological tradition is that scientific analysis of quantitative results is to gain insights into the working of individual minds—that is, "into the causal processes presumed to govern the psychological functioning of a person" (Lamiell, 1995, p. 144). The quantitative methods were applied to the analysis of multiple observations made on individual subjects. The intensive study of individual participants was viewed as an essential step to the generation of nomothetic knowledge. Generality was sought through replication across participants, which was the method used to generate nomothetic knowledge as defined by Windelband. However, near the beginning of the 20th century, psychologists were attempting to base their definition of psychology on a positivist philosophy of science. Key concepts in Wundt's psychology were rejected as metaphysical, and the Leipzig research model was rejected (Danziger, 1979).

Clinical Experiment Research Model

During the development of the Leipzig model of experimentation in Germany, another, different research model was developing among medical researchers in France. An important conceptual change occurred at this time. Instead of viewing participants as "independently functioning psychological entities" (Lamiell, 1995, p. 144), researchers viewed them as psychological "categories" (e.g., "hysteric" or "psychotic").

> In a subtle but profound way, the focus had shifted from an interest in knowledge about *persons* to a concern for knowledge about *variables*. This would inevitably entail the lumping together, for research purposes, of individuals differing from one another in countless respects but sharing a medically diagnostic label. (Lamiell, 1995, p. 144)

The clinical experiment model attempted to determine the effectiveness of a particular treatment by studying the effectiveness of the treatment, on average, for persons suffering from a particular illness.

Criticisms of this approach were made almost from the outset (for details, see Danziger, 1990; Porter, 1986):

> We learn from this that very early on in the course of methodological developments that would have a profound and lasting impact on research practice within psychology, there were scholars who were distinguishing between the *use of aggregate statistics,* on the one hand, and the *achievement of scientific generalities,* on the other. Though this distinction was respected by the Leipzig model, it was blurred as the clinical experiment model rose to favour, and has been fairly well obliterated by subsequent generations of psychological researchers. (Lamiell, 1995, p. 145)

Galton Research Model

According to Danziger, the Galton model eventually gave shape to the development of the individual-difference approach in psychology. Instead of viewing deviations from the mean as "errors of nature," as advocated by the Belgian statistician Adolphe Quételet (1835), researchers viewed these differences as biologically determined differences among humans. Instead of the assumption that these differences were errors of nature, as argued by Quételet (1835), Galton's ontological assumption was that these differences were a mirror of nature. These assumptions, Galton argued, were congruent with Darwin's theory of evolution:

> While the clinical experiment model and the Galton model differed in certain respects, they shared in common the view that *participant aggregates*—and not *participants*—were the proper units of investigation. Within the clinical experiment model, for example, a statement about "hysterics" or "somnambulists" would be a statement about the *average* value of some variable within a *group* of persons so diagnosed, and not about any particular person so diagnosed. Similarly within the Galton (individual differences) model, the correlation between, say, IQ and speed of reaction to auditory stimuli is a numerical value definable for a *group* (sample, population) of persons, and not for any individual person within that group. (Lamiell, 1995, pp. 145–146)

The clinical experiment approach and Galton's model were different from the Leipzig model, which stipulated that the proper unit of investigation was the person. Due to its emphasis on introspection and due to socio-historico-political reasons, the Leipzig research model practically disappeared (for details, see Danziger, 1990; Gigerenzer et al., 1989; Rucci & Tweeney, 1980). Both the clinical experiment model and the Galton individual-difference model survived and became the ancestors of what Cronbach (1957, 1975) termed the *two disciplines of scientific psychology.*

A consequence of this methodological development is that today many researchers assume that the frontiers of scientific psychology are best pushed back by using the significance testing approach in which data are aggregated among participants. This approach is frequently applied to measures of central tendency (group means), dispersion (group variance), and association between variables (correlation).

CHANGING PERSPECTIVES ABOUT PERSONS WITH A DISABILITY

Attitudes, perceptions, and treatment of persons with a disability over the last 150 years have been guided by several ideologies. In this section, I give a brief overview of changes in perceptions, attitudes, and treatment of persons labeled *mentally handicapped.* It is important to note that these changes were often due more to crusades than debates, and crusades are little affected by evidence and logic. In North America, it is possible to distinguish five major trends.

Between 1850 and 1880, it was believed that persons with a disability had to be separated from society for some time in order to be rehabilitated and then returned to society. The purpose of working with persons with a developmental disability was to make them "normal." It was assumed that an isolation period was necessary to protect the person with a disability from society and that separating mentally handicapped persons from the community was the best way to prevent society from taking unfair advantage of them (Deutsch & Bustow, 1982).

With the advent of the eugenics movement toward the end of the 19th century, societal responses to persons with disabilities began to change drastically. The period 1880–1950 was marked by an increase in the number of facility-based services like institutions, residential programs, and to a certain extent, special schools. Instead of protecting persons with disabilities from society, the new ideology was to protect society from persons with disabilities. Lewis Terman (1916), a pioneer of the IQ testing movement in North America, wrote that "there is no investigator who denies the fearful role played by mental deficiency in the production of vice, crime, and delinquency" (cited in Kamin, 1995). Henry Goddard, often viewed as the father of the eugenics movement, had ideas that were not substantially different from Terman's. Both Goddard and Terman assumed that "weak-mindedness" was a product of Mendelian inheritance and therefore was not alterable. To protect society from mentally handicapped persons, Goddard believed that the cure for mental retardation, and a method of preventing additional mentally retarded persons from being born, was to segregate the retarded from society or to sterilize them (Deutsch & Bustow, 1982). Such beliefs and ideologies led to dehumanization and long-term institutionalization of mentally handicapped persons.

The late 1950s and early 1960s raised awareness about the treatment mentally handicapped persons were receiving in institutions. A shocked public became aware of behaviors like headbanging, crying, biting, vomiting, assaulting, screeching, rocking, and sleeping observed in overcrowded institutions (Blatt, 1987). A movement toward deinstitutionalisation and normalization began, and the services-based model gained momentum (Polloway, J. D. Smith, Patton, & T. E. C. Smith, 1996). This model provided special services to persons with a disability as a preparation for their integration into society. The assumption was made that the provision of special segregated services for persons with a disability would be followed by successful integration into society (Polloway et al., 1996). However, the model was quickly perceived as ineffective in returning persons with a disability to society. In reality, many students remained in special classes, year after year; "transitional" group homes became permanent residences; and sheltered workshops were frequently the final vocational placement (Polloway et al., 1996).

In reaction to the inefficiency of the services-based model, a support-based inclusion model emerged during the 1980s. Under a support-based model, the assumption is made that "individuals should be maintained in inclusive settings and supported in those locations in order to insure successful learning, work experiences, and/or adjustment" (Polloway et al., 1996, p. 6). This model assumes that placement begins in an ecologically valid setting, and plans are made to ensure its success through the provision of appropriate and necessary supports. This concept of inclusion stipulates that each person, regardless of his or her abilities, has the right to participate actively in natural settings within his or her community (Polloway et al., 1996). In terms of physical education within the school system, inclusion means that persons with a disability are placed into regular physical education classes from the beginning (Block, 1994).

The previous models can be viewed as dependency models in which experts are providing services to clients. In these dependency models, professionals often make decisions, or at least recommendations, for their clients. Perusal of the inclusion literature in the 1990s clearly indicates a tendency to abandon dependency models. The concepts of empowerment, self-determination, autonomy, self-realization, and self-regulation are beginning to drive the present ideology (Brotherson, C. C. Cook, Cunconan-Lahr, & Wehmeyer, 1995; Polloway et al., 1996; Sands & Doll, 1996; Wehmeyer, 1992; Wehmeyer, Kelcher, & Richards, 1996). These concepts emphasize that persons with a disability should have more freedom to make personal decisions about their lives. This is likely to be a challenging task in the area of mental retardation—an area in which people have often been dependent on others to make decisions.

IMPLICATIONS AND FUTURE DIRECTIONS

As noted earlier, recurrent themes in the adapted physical activity field are captured by expressions like *empowerment, self-determination, self-actualization,* and *self-*

regulation. Common to all these constructs is the idea that persons with a disability should have the opportunity and freedom to make choices. Instead of having their lives determined by others, persons with a disability should have the opportunity to be the causal agents determining what happens to them.

To illustrate the implications for research practice of this relatively recent ideology in the adapted physical activity field, I borrow extensively from our research program on self-regulated learning of movement skills presently being conducted at the University of Alberta (Bouffard & Dunn, 1993; Bouffard, Romanow, With, & Peterson, 1995). Although the present program focuses on the study of self-regulated learning of movement skills, the conceptual framework guiding our research can easily be extended to other domains of research.

Most theories of self-regulation recognize three general aspects of self-regulated learning—attempts by the learner to control his or her behavior, cognition, and motivation and affect (Pintrich, 1995). *Self-regulation of behavior* involves the learner's active control of his or her various resources (e.g., study time, learning environment, instruments that might facilitate learning; Pintrich, 1995). *Self-regulation of cognition* involves the learner's control of several cognitive strategies for learning. These strategies could be divided into lower level strategies (e.g., imaging, labeling, counting) and higher level strategies that help the learner control learning or thinking (e.g., planning, monitoring, evaluating; Schraw & Moshman, 1995). *Self-regulation of motivational beliefs* (e.g., efficacy or goal orientation) is frequently recognized, explicitly or implicitly, as a determinant of self-regulatory behavior (Borkowski & Thorpe, 1994; Meece, 1994; Pintrich, 1995; Schunk, 1994). Motivational beliefs are included in most self-regulation theories. It is becoming increasingly clear that only someone who intends to be personally responsible for reaching a certain goal will use adequate processing and regulation components. Although the regulation of emotion and motivation is a key component of self-regulation, this aspect has not been explicitly studied in our research program yet.

Goal pursuit plays a central role in numerous self-regulation theories (Baumeister, Heatherton, & Tice, 1994; Butler & Winne, 1995; Carver & Scheier, 1981, 1982; Karoly, 1993; Mithaug, 1993). Much of the research and theories of self-regulation have borrowed extensively from systems theory, particularly the concept of feedback loops (Butler & Winne, 1995; Carver & Scheier, 1981, 1982; Mithaug, 1993; Nelson, 1996; Schunk & Zimmerman, 1994). A key assumption of these theories is that self-regulatory behavior is a function of the perception of a discrepancy between a goal state and a current state (Mithaug, 1993). These theories assume that central to self-regulation is a comparison of the desired goal against the actual state. If a mismatch is perceived, a new operation is completed before another test is conducted. This sequence is repeated until there is no perceived discrepancy between actual state and desired goal.

To self-regulate behavior, then, the goal state to be achieved must be clear. A person who does not have a clear standard cannot have any basis for self-regulation

(Baumeister et al., 1994; Karoly, 1993). From this viewpoint, self-regulation failure may occur when the learning goal is misunderstood. From a research perspective, lack of congruence between the goal understood by the teacher or experimenter and the goal state of the subject might compromise any examination of self-regulation that follows. If the goal state is clear, self-regulation failure might be due to nonuse of self-checking strategies. *Self-checking strategies* refers to optional cognitive processes or actions that might allow the learner to determine whether the goal has been reached or not. To monitor their own behavior, learners can use self-checking strategies to discover what they have done correctly and incorrectly. A learner who does not use self-checking strategies does not conduct a crucial test comparing actual state against desired goal. Hence, self-regulation failure could be observed (Baumeister et al., 1994).

The use of self-checking strategies per se does not ensure quality self-regulation. The ability to detect errors is central to self-regulation. As Zimmerman (1994) noted, "It appears that the accuracy of one's self-monitoring directly influences one's capability to self-regulate performance outcomes" (p. 12). The perceptions people have of their own knowledge state determines how they allocate their time and energy in a learning situation. If the judgments of movement reproduction accuracy (error detection) made by the learner are of poor quality, this could restrict planning decisions, movement outcomes, and error corrections.

This brief survey of key concepts in self-regulation theories, and the comments made earlier, has several research implications. In order to study self-regulated learning, the learner must be given personal choice and freedom: Inferences about students' self-regulation "cannot be made if they do not have options available or cannot control an essential dimension of their learning, such as one's method of studying" (Zimmerman, 1994, p. 6). From this standpoint, the learner should be free to make decisions about the learning process. Consequently, research methods in which the researcher attempts to control what the learner is doing are likely to be inadequate to study self-regulation. Experimenter control of the learning process is equivalent to the assignment of the executive function to the experimenter rather than to the subject (Belmont & Butterfield, 1977) and consequently is incompatible with the study of self-regulation.

Completion of intensive studies of individuals is essential to the study of self-regulation. Although the motor-learning field shifted away from a "product-oriented approach" to a "process-oriented approach" during the early 1970s (Schmidt, 1976), the learner's cognitive processes have usually been inferred post hoc from the (usually quantitative) products they produced (Winne, 1982). These products have usually been obtained by aggregating data over groups of people. Such aggregation may obscure individual differences in cognitive processes (Bouffard, 1993). Better assessment procedures of these processes are essential in order to foster progress.

A potentially fruitful research method to develop a model of self-directed learning in movement situations is the use of an online microgenetic approach

(Siegler & Crowley, 1991). The key features of this approach are that (a) observations span the entire learning episode, (b) "the density of observation is high relative to the rate of change of the phenomena, [and] (c) observed behavior is subjected to intensive trial-by-trial analysis, with the goal of inferring the processes that give rise to both quantitative and qualitative aspects of change" (Siegler & Crowley, 1991, p. 606).

Psychological investigations conducted on cognitive processes used by subjects while learning have revealed substantial variability both across and within subjects. Battig (1975) demonstrated within-individual differences on serial learning, paired-associates learning, verbal-discrimination learning, and free recall. Battig was able to show that different people use different processes on the same task and that each subject uses different processes on different trials and even on different items within single trials. Similar findings were obtained by Siegler (1987; Siegler & J. Campbell, 1990). By using the microgenetic approach, Siegler demonstrated substantial intra-individual differences, with a given child using a variety of strategies depending on the difficulty of the arithmetic problem. In addition, Siegler (1987) showed that inferences arrived at by aggregating over groups of children did not reflect how an individual child solved a problem.

Self-regulation studies completed in our laboratory have shown substantial variability both between subjects and within subjects in processes used to learn movement sequences (Bouffard & Dunn, 1993; Bouffard et al., 1995). In several studies, children were asked to learn movement sequences presented by a model on a videotape. A recall-readiness paradigm was used in which the participants were shown a sequence and were informed that they were free to study the sequence for as long as they wanted and to do whatever they wanted in order to learn it. When the child felt the sequence was learned, he or she informed the experimenter, who then asked the participant to perform the sequence without the model. The learning episodes were videotaped, and the tapes were coded using a timed-event sequential-data coding procedure in which the coder records both the onset and offset times of each event (Bakeman & Quera, 1995).

To capture possible strategy changes over time, the sequential learning data were divided into three segments of approximately equal length for each participant. SDIS–GSEQ, software specifically designed for the analysis of sequential data (Bakeman & Quera, 1995), was used to obtain the total time each strategy was used during each segment. The data have shown considerable variability in strategies used both among participants and within participants over time. Further, preliminary analysis of the data suggests that the best learners use different distributions of strategies over time. The discovery of these intra-individual and interindividual differences was made possible by the intensive study of each participant's learning episode.

In agreement with several philosophers of science and research methodologists (e.g., see Bogdan, 1994; Borg & Gall, 1983; M. L. Smith & Glass, 1987; Trigg,

1993), researchers are attempting to build models or theories of the natural or social world surrounding them. To this effect, the collection of empirical information is used either to discover or justify models and theories. To ignore the methods used by the participants in self-regulation studies can only lead to confusion and incomplete results (Newell, 1973). No matter

> where or how it is evaluated, any theory or model may well be both entirely correct or totally wrong, depending upon what type(s) of processing the particular subject happens to be using for a given item within a particular task. (Battig, 1975, p. 225)

MEASUREMENT, STATISTICS, AND RESEARCH DESIGN NEEDS OF THE FUTURE

Researchers need to ask a fundamental question: *"What are the entities over which generality/universality is being sought or asserted?"* (Lamiell, 1987, p. 14). Dependent on the purpose of the researcher, the research can be strictly idiographic (limited to one person) or nomothetic (Nesselroade & Ford, 1985). If the research question is asked about one person, then data should be collected on that one person; if the question is more general with respect to persons, then data should be collected on more than one subject (Nesselroade & Ford, 1985).

Adapted physical activity researchers should seriously consider first completing idiographic studies. To generate nomothetic knowledge, the research style advocated here should follow replication-across-people logic instead of sampling logic. This means that two or more cases should be included within the same study precisely because the investigator predicts that similar results (replications) will be found. If the same functional relationship is found between two persons, then the study should be replicated with a third person, and so on (Sidman, 1960). If such replications are indeed found for several cases, then confidence in the overall results increases. Claims for generality can be supported by replicating the study with more participants. We should remember that medical science has largely depended on the accumulation of intrasystemic knowledge through case studies and their replication (Valsiner, 1986b). The development of consistent findings over multiple cases and even over multiple studies can then be considered a very robust finding.

Replication logic is different from sampling logic. Sampling logic assumes that an investigation is mainly interested in "representing" a larger universe. The participants selected are therefore chosen according to preidentified representation criteria. Replication logic is a method to test the generality of statements—to discover nomothetic regularities.

In conclusion, I suggest measurement, research design, and statistics problems that need to be addressed in order to ultimately study self-empowerment and self-regulation. Central to most self-regulation theories is a comparison of the desired state against the actual state. To assess the desired state, researchers must know which goals are pursued by the participant. How can we better assess people's goals when the literature suggests that the goals are often fleeting and fluctuating? This is likely to be a challenging task, especially with developmentally delayed persons. Assessment of the actual state most likely implies that the participants' perceptual capabilities must be assessed. How can we assess people's error-detection capabilities? I know that some work has been completed with simple end-position movements. However, I do not know any work completed with gross, ecologically valid movements. Further, how can we assess error-detection capabilities during the unfolding of movements?

If we accept Battig's (1975) contention that the results obtained in a study can be entirely dependent on the processes used by the participant, how can we assess the processes and strategies used by participants to regulate their own behavior? One possible avenue is to make inferences from observable behavior. It is obvious that the plausibility of inferences made from behavior needs evidential support. Use of direct observation of behavior, however, cannot reflect all of the covert processes a participant might use (e.g., imagery, labeling). In this case, the use of verbal reports to supplement direct observation might be the best research avenue. Following the work of Siegler and Crowley (1992), I suggest that direct observation of behavior in combination with verbal report and/or retrospective report (Ericsson & Simon, 1993) might allow for the assessment of strategies that would otherwise go undetected.

The validity of inferences made from verbal report has been controversial and problematic (e.g., see Ericsson & Simon, 1993; Nisbett & Wilson, 1977). The plausibility of inferences made from self-report can be documented on both theoretical and empirical grounds. On theoretical grounds, because our research program on self-regulation focuses on the early or cognitive stage (Fitts & Posner, 1967) of skill acquisition, the validity of self-report is likely to be higher than it would be if the skill were already automatic (Abernethy, K. T. Thomas, & J. T. Thomas, 1993). The cognitive stage is usually recognized as very conscious, serial, deliberate, and effortful (Adams, 1971; Fitts & Posner, 1967; Gentile, 1987), and hence facilitates the report of thoughts. Some examples in support of this contention are the beginner driver who can reliably report each of the steps involved in changing gears and the beginning typist who can accurately describe the position of the fingers on the keyboard. Further, the accuracy of verbal reports is higher when the focus of verbal report is on movement selection instead of movement execution. In a recent review on motor expertise, Abernethy et al. (1993) concluded that the accessibility of procedural knowledge might be more prevalent when sport researchers are examining movement-selection processes compared to movement-execution processes, especially when examining the decision-making elements of high-strategy motor tasks.

Tools for the statistical analysis of sequential data need to be imported into our field, and their relevance to answer our research questions needs to be assessed. I believe that a major contribution of statistics to research and evaluation has been in discovering or confirming patterns. It is obvious that the microgenetic approach can produce massive amounts of data. Researchers will need tools to facilitate the analysis of both qualitative and quantitative data. A study of the relevance of some tools already available in ethology (Haccou & Meelis, 1992) and psychology (Wickens, 1982), as well as within-person correlational designs (Michela, 1990), might be a good place to start.

ACKNOWLEDGMENTS

Preparation of this article was supported by Social Sciences and Humanities Research Council of Canada Grant 410–95–0970.

REFERENCES

Abernethy, B., Thomas, K. T., & Thomas, J. T. (1993). Strategies for improving understanding of motor expertise [or mistakes we have made and things we have learned!!]. In J. L. Starkes & F. Allard (Eds.), *Cognitive issues in motor expertise* (pp. 317–356). Amsterdam: North-Holland.

Adams, J. A. (1971). A closed-loop theory of motor learning. *Journal of Motor Behavior, 3,* 111–149.

Allport, G. W. (1962). The general and the unique in psychological science. *Journal of Personality, 30,* 405–422.

Angeles, P. A. (1981). *Dictionary of philosophy.* New York: Barnes & Noble.

Bakeman, R., & Quera, V. (1995). *Analyzing interaction: Sequential analysis with SDIS and GSEQ.* New York: Cambridge University Press.

Barlow, D. H., & Hersen, M. (1984). *Single case experimental designs: Strategies for studying behavioral change* (2nd ed.). New York: Permagon.

Battig, W. F. (1975). Within-individual differences in "cognitive" processes. In R. L. Solso (Ed.), *Information processing and cognition: The Loyola Symposium* (pp. 195–228). Hillsdale, NJ: Lawrence Erlbaum Associates, Inc.

Baumeister, R. F., Heatherton, T. D., & Tice, D. M. (1994). *Losing control: How and why people fail at self-regulation.* San Diego: Academic.

Belmont, J. M., & Butterfield, E. C. (1977). The instructional approach to developmental cognitive research. In R. V. Kail, Jr. & J. W. Hagen (Eds.), *Perspectives on the development of memory and cognition* (pp. 437–481). Hillsdale, NJ: Lawrence Erlbaum Associates, Inc.

Blatt, B. (1987). *The conquest of mental retardation.* Austin, TX: Pro-Ed.

Block, M. E. (1994). *A teacher's guide to including students with disabilities in regular physical education.* Baltimore, MD: Brookes.

Bogdan, R. J. (1994). *Grounds for cognition: How goal-directed behavior shapes the mind.* Hillsdale, NJ: Lawrence Erlbaum Associates, Inc.

Borg, W. R., & Gall, M. D. (1983). *Educational research: An introduction* (4th ed.). New York: Longman.

Borkowski, J. G., & Thorpe, P. K. (1994). Self-regulation and motivation: A life-span perspective on underachievement. In D. H. Schunk & B. J. Zimmerman (Eds.), *Self-regulation of learning and performance: Issues and educational applications* (pp. 45–73). Hillsdale, NJ: Lawrence Erlbaum Associates, Inc.

Bouffard, M. (1993). The perils of averaging data in adapted physical activity research. *Adapted Physical Activity Quarterly, 10,* 371–391.

Bouffard, M., & Dunn, J. G. H. (1993). Children's self-regulated learning of movement sequences. *Research Quarterly for Exercise and Sport, 64,* 393–403.

Bouffard, M., Romanow, S. K. E., With, T., & Peterson, T. (1995, October). *Moving toward independence: A microgenetic approach to self-directed movement learning.* Symposium conducted at the meeting of the Canadian Society for Psychomotor Learning and Sport Psychology, Vancouver, Canada.

Brotherson, M. J., Cook, C. C., Cunconan-Lahr, R., & Wehmeyer, M. L. (1995, March). Policy supporting self-determination in the environments of children with disabilities. *Education and Training in Mental Retardation and Developmental Disabilities, 30,* 3–14.

Butler, D. L., & Winne, P. H. (1995). Feedback and self-regulated learning: A theoretical synthesis. *Review of Educational Research, 65,* 245–281.

Campbell, D. T., & Stanley, J. C. (1963). *Experimental and quasi-experimental designs for research.* Chicago: Rand McNally.

Carver, C. S., & Scheier, M. F. (1981). *Attention and self-regulation: A control theory appproach to human behavior.* New York: Springer-Verlag.

Carver, C. S., & Scheier, M. F. (1982). Control theory: A useful conceptual framework for personality—Social, clinical and health psychology. *Psychological Bulletin, 92,* 111–135.

Cook, T. D., & Campbell, D. T. (1979). *Quasi-experimentation: Design and analysis issues for field settings.* Chicago: Rand McNally.

Cronbach, L. J. (1957). The two disciplines of scientific psychology. *American Psychologist, 12,* 671–684.

Cronbach, L. J. (1975). Beyond the two disciplines of scientific psychology. *American Psychologist, 30,* 116–127.

Danziger, K. (1979). The positivist repudiation of Wundt. *Journal of the History of the Behavioral Sciences, 15,* 205–230.

Danziger, K. (1987). Statistical methods and the historical development of research practice in American psychology. In L. Kruger, G. Gigerenzer, & M. S. Morgan (Eds.), *Ideas in the sciences: Vol. 2. The probabilistic revolution* (pp. 35–47). Cambridge, MA: MIT Press.

Danziger, K. (1990). *Constructing the subject.* New York: Cambridge University Press.

Darlington, R. B. (1990). *Regression and linear models.* New York: McGraw-Hill.

Deutsch, H., & Bustow, S. (1982). *Developmental disabilities: A training guide.* Boston: CBI.

Ericsson, K. A., & Simon, H. A. (1993). *Protocol analysis: Verbal reports as data* (Rev. ed.). Cambridge, MA: MIT Press.

Fitts, P. M., & Posner, M. I. (1967). *Human performance.* Belmont, CA: Brooks/Cole.

Frank, I. (1986). Psychology as a science: Resolving the idiographic–nomothetic controversy. In J. Valsiner (Ed.), *The individual subject and scientific psychology* (pp. 17–36). New York: Plenum.

Gentile, A. M. (1987). Skill acquisition: Action, movement, and neuromotor processes. In J. H. Carr, R. B. Shepherd, J. Gordon, A. M. Gentile, & J. M. Held (Eds.), *Movement science: Foundations for physical therapy in rehabilitation* (pp. 93–154). Rockville, MD: Aspen.

Gigerenzer, G., Swijtink, Z., Porter, T., Daston, L., Beatty, J., Krüger, L. (1989). *The empire of chance.* New York: Cambridge University Press.

Haccou, P., & Meelis, E. (1992). *Statistical analysis of behavioural data: An approach based on time-structured models.* Oxford, England: Oxford University Press.

Holton, G. (1988). *Thematic origins of scientific thought: Kepler to Einstein* (Rev. ed.). Cambridge, MA: Harvard University Press.

Hume, D. (1888). *A treatise of human nature.* Oxford, England: Clarendon. (Original work published 1740).

Kamin, L. J. (1995). The pioneers of IQ testing. In R. Jacobi & N. Glauberman (Eds.), *The bell curve debate: History, documents, opinions* (pp. 476–509). New York: Times Books.

Kaplan, A. (1964). *The conduct of inquiry: Methodology for the behavioral science.* New York: Harper & Row.

Karoly, P. (1993). Mechanisms of self-regulation: A systems view. *Annual Review of Psychology, 44,* 23–52.

Kirk, R. E. (1982). *Experimental design* (2nd ed.). Belmont, CA: Brooks/Cole.

Kratochwill, T. R., & Levin, J. R. (Eds.). (1992). *Single-case research design and analysis: New directions for psychology and education.* Hillsdale, NJ: Lawrence Erlbaum Associates, Inc.

Lamiell, J. T. (1987). *The psychology of personality.* New York: Columbia University Press.

Lamiell, J. T. (1991). Valuation theory, the self-confrontation method, and scientific personality psychology. *European Journal of Personality, 5,* 235–244.

Lamiell, J. T. (1995). Rethinking the role of quantitative methods in psychology. In J. A. Smith, R. Harré, & L. Van Langenhove (Eds.), *Rethinking methods in psychology* (pp. 143–161). Thousand Oaks, CA: Sage.

Maxwell, S. E., & Delaney, H. D. (1990). *Designing experiments and analyzing data: A model comparison perspective.* Belmont, CA: Wadsworth.

Meece, J. L. (1994). The role of motivation in self-regulated learning. In D. H. Schunk & B. J. Zimmerman (Eds.), *Self-regulation of learning and performance: Issues and educational applications* (pp. 25–44). Hillsdale, NJ: Lawrence Erlbaum Associates, Inc.

Michela, J. L. (1990). Within-person correlational design and analysis. In C. Hendrick & M. S. Clark (Eds.), *Research methods in personality and social psychology* (pp. 279–311). Newbury Park, CA: Sage.

Mithaug, D. E. (1993). *Self-regulation theory: How optimal adjustment maximizes gain.* Westport, CT: Praeger.

Mueller, R. O. (1996). *Basic principles of structural equation modeling.* New York: Springer.

Nelson, T. O. (1996). Consciousness and metacognition. *American Psychologist, 51,* 102–116.

Nesselroade, J. R., & Ford, D. H. (1985). P-technique comes of age: Multivariate, replicated, single-subject designs for research on older adults. *Research on Aging, 7,* 46–80.

Newell, A. (1973). You can't play 20 questions with nature and win: Projective comments on the papers of this symposium. In W. G. Chase (Ed.), *Visual information processing* (pp. 283–308). New York: Academic.

Nisbett, R. E., & Wilson, T. D. (1977). Telling more than we can know: Verbal report on mental processes. *Psychological Review, 84,* 231–259.

Nunnally, J. C. (1978). *Psychometric theory* (2nd ed.). New York: McGraw-Hill.

Pintrich, P. R. (1995). Understanding self-regulated learning. In P. R. Pintrich (Ed.), *Understanding self-regulated learning* (pp. 3–12). San Francisco: Jossey-Bass.

Polloway, E. A., Smith, J. D., Patton, J. R., & Smith, T. E. C. (1996, March). Historic changes in mental retardation and developmental disabilities. *Education and Training in Mental Retardation and Developmental Disabilities, 31,* 3–12.

Porter, T. M. (1986). *The rise of statistical thinking: 1820–1900.* Princeton, NJ: Princeton University Press.

Quételet, A. (1835). *Sur l'homme et le développement de ses facultés, ou Essai de physique sociale* [A treatise on man and the development of his faculties]. Paris: Bachelier.

Rucci, A. J., & Tweeney, R. D. (1980). Analysis of variance and the "second discipline" of scientific psychology: A historical account. *Psychological Bulletin, 87,* 166–184.

Sands, D. J., & Doll, B. (1996). Fostering self-determination is a developmental task. *Journal of Special Education, 30,* 58–76.

Schmidt, R. A. (1976). The schema as a solution to some persistent problems in motor learning. In G. E. Stelmach (Ed.), *Motor control: Issues and trends* (pp. 41–65). New York: Academic.

Schraw, G., & Moshman, D. (1995). Metacognitive theories. *Educational Psychology Review, 7,* 351–371.

Schunk, D. H. (1994). Self-regulation of self-efficacy and attributions in academic settings. In D. H. Schunk & B. J. Zimmerman (Eds.), *Self-regulation of learning and performance: Issues and educational applications* (pp. 75–99). Hillsdale, NJ: Lawrence Erlbaum Associates, Inc.

Schunk, D. H., & Zimmerman, B. J. (Eds.). (1994). *Self-regulation of learning and performance: Issues and educational applications.* Hillsdale, NJ: Lawrence Erlbaum Associates, Inc.

Sidman, M. (1960). *Tactics of scientific research.* New York: Basic.

Siegler, R. S. (1987). The perils of averaging data over strategies: An example from children's addition. *Journal of Experimental Psychology: General, 116,* 250–264.

Siegler, R. S., & Campbell, J. (1990). Diagnosing individual differences in strategy choice procedures. In N. Frederiksen, R. Glaser, A. Lesgold, & M. G. Shafto (Eds.), *Diagnostic monitoring of skill and knowledge acquisition* (pp. 113–139). Hillsdale, NJ: Lawrence Erlbaum Associates, Inc.

Siegler, R. S., & Crowley, K. (1991). The microgenetic method: A direct method for studying cognitive development. *American Psychologist, 46,* 606–620.

Siegler, R. S., & Crowley, K. (1992). Microgenetic methods revisited. *American Psychologist, 47,* 1241–1243.

Smith, M. L., & Glass, G. V. (1987). *Research and evaluation in education and the social sciences.* Englewood Cliffs, NJ: Prentice Hall.

Terman, L. M. (1916). *The measurement of intelligence.* Boston: Houghton Mifflin.

Thorndike, R. M. (1978). *Correlational procedures for research.* New York: Gardner.

Trigg, R. (1993). *Rationality and science: Can science explain everything?* Cambridge, MA: Blackwell.

Valsiner, J. (Ed.). (1986a). *The individual subject and scientific psychology.* New York: Plenum.

Valsiner, J. (1986b). Where is the individual in scientific psychology? In J. Valsiner (Ed.), *The individual subject and scientific psychology* (pp. 1–14). New York: Plenum.

Wehmeyer, M. L. (1992, December). Self-determination and the education of students with mental retardation. *Education and Training in Mental Retardation, 27,* 302–314.

Wehmeyer, M. L., Kelcher, K., & Richards, S. (1996). Essential characteristics of self-determined behavior of individuals with mental retardation. *American Journal on Mental Retardation, 100,* 632–642.

Wickens, T. D. (1982). *Models for behavior: Stochastic processes in psychology.* San Francisco: Freeman.

Windelband, W. (1904). *Geschichte und Naturwissenschaft* [History and natural science] (3rd ed.). Strasburg, Germany: Heitz.

Winer, B. J. (1971). *Statistical principles in experimental design* (2nd ed.). New York: McGraw-Hill.

Winne, P. H. (1982). Minimizing the black box problem to enhance the validity of theories about instructional effects. *Instructional Science, 11,* 13–28.

Wottawa, H. (1990). Idiographic versus nomothetic methodology. In J. Brzezinski & T. Marek (Eds.), *Action and performance: Models and tests* (pp. 67–76). Amsterdam: Rodopi.

Yin, R. K. (1989). *Case study research: Design and methods* (Rev. ed.). Newbury Park, CA: Sage.

Zimmermann, B. J. (1994). Dimensions of academic self-regulation: A conceptual framework for education. In D. H. Schunk & B. J. Zimmerman (Eds.), *Self-regulation of learning and performance: Issues and educational applications* (pp. 3–21). Hillsdale, NJ: Lawrence Erlbaum Associates, Inc.

MEASUREMENT IN PHYSICAL EDUCATION AND EXERCISE SCIENCE, 1(1), 89–102

Estimating Sample Size in Repeated-Measures Analysis of Variance

Zung Vu Tran

Center for Research in Ambulatory Health Care Administration
Medical Group Management Association
Englewood, Colorado

The problems of estimating appropriate sample size and associated power for conducting experiments have received ample attention in the statistical literature (Cohen, 1988; Donner, 1984; Fleiss, 1986; Hsieh, 1989; Lachin, 1981; Moher, Dulberg, & Wells, 1994; Rochon, 1991; van Belle & Martin, 1993). This literature covers many statistical models, from t test to multiple logistic regression. The ineffectiveness of this literature in changing investigators' behavior is a subject that has also been discussed in the research literature. Although it is not the intent of this article to cover in any detail the history of this apparent inattention to power by consumers of statistical methodology (e.g., researchers in the various subdisciplines of exercise science), these issues do merit a brief review. A review of the statistical issues surrounding power is also warranted to set the stage for the discussion of estimating sample size and associated power for repeated-measures analysis of variance (ANOVA).

REVIEW OF ISSUES RELATED TO POWER

Type I and Type II Errors

The level of significance of a statistical test, alpha (α), or the probability of a Type I error, is a familiar concept. This is the probability of falsely rejecting the null

Requests for reprints should be sent to Zung Vu Tran, Center for Research in Ambulatory Health Care Administration, Medical Group Management Association, 104 Inverness Terrace East, Englewood, CO 80112–5306. E-mail: ztran@mgma.com.

hypothesis (H_0) when it is true (i.e., concluding that groups differ when they actually do not). Acceptable alpha levels, set by the investigator, are subjective decisions and are usually set at either 5% or 1% (although there are situations in which 10% or even 15% might be a reasonable or acceptable level). These alpha levels focus on minimizing the probability of making a Type I error. Another type of error that can be made when performing a statistical test is a Type II error or beta (β). This is the probability of falsely accepting the null hypothesis (i.e., concluding that groups do not differ when they actually do).

Added to the fact that either type of error might occur in the course of making a decision about the outcomes of an experiment is the probability that these errors are inversely related. That is, as we decrease the acceptable level of a Type I error (making alpha smaller), the probability of a Type II error will increase. This is illustrated by examining the t distribution shown in Figure 1.

If alpha is set at 1% (and sample size is set at $n = 10$/group), then the calculated t statistic needed to exceed the "critical value" is 3.355 (where a difference may be deemed statistically significant at $\alpha = 1\%$). However, if alpha is 5%, then the t statistic needed is smaller (2.306). This smaller value is more readily exceeded and corresponds to having more power to say that there is a difference between two groups. That is, a smaller difference between groups is needed to conclude that there is a statistically significant difference. Thus, the problem for an investigator planning an experiment is to achieve an appropriate balance between the two types of error. Unfortunately, even though the literature is well developed, investigators have tended to neglect Type II errors (and thus power) in favor of controlling Type I errors.

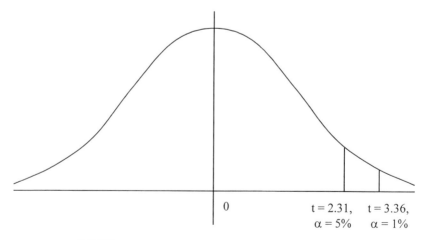

$$0$$

$$t = 2.31, \quad t = 3.36,$$
$$\alpha = 5\% \quad \alpha = 1\%$$

FIGURE 1   Critical values for t distribution ($\alpha = 5\%$ vs. $\alpha = 1\%$).

Power

The power of a statistical test is dependent on many factors such as reliability of the dependent measure, sample size, alpha level, effect size, and intra-individual and interindividual variability. Three factors, however, are conveniently manipulated by the investigator—alpha level, sample size, and effect size. Briefly, effect size is the expected difference between two groups as a result of an intervention. For our discussion, effect size = $(\mu_1 - \mu_2) / \sigma$, where σ is the assumed common population standard deviation (Glass, McGaw, & Smith, 1981). Thus, effect size indicates the degree of difference between the two groups in standard deviation units or the standardized effect.

Other things being equal, power is heavily dependent on sample size (Stevens, 1992). However, this dependency is reduced when sample size exceeds 60. As can be seen in Figure 2, there is a proportionate increase in power with increasing sample sizes up to about 60. At this point, increases in sample sizes do not elicit a proportionate return in power.

Neglect of Power

Sedlmeier and Gigerenzer (1989), using Cohen's (1962) pioneering work as a model, studied the long-term impact of studies of statistical power on the power of subsequently published research studies. Confining their analysis to the psychological literature, they concluded that, in the 24 years since Cohen's (1962) work, there had been no impact. Cohen analyzed all studies published in the 1960 volume of the *Journal of Abnormal and Social Psychology,* finding that the median power (for a medium-size effect) was 46%. Analyzing the same journal 24 years later, Sedlmeier and Gigerenzer found the median power to be 37%, and they indicated that the possibility of low power seemed to have been ignored, with only 2 of 64 studies even mentioning power. Further, power was never estimated. Nonsignificant findings were generally interpreted as confirmation of the null hypothesis even though, in the subset of studies with nonsignificant findings, the median power was 25%.

More recently, Cohen (1992) reexamined this apparent neglect of statistical power. Cohen (1962) had originally attributed this neglect to the "inaccessibility of a meager and mathematically difficult literature" (Cohen, 1992, p. 155). The first edition of his power handbook (Cohen, 1969) was intended to address this problem. The most current edition of this handbook was published in 1988. In this more recent publication, his solution was again to provide even more convenient (but not as comprehensive) sample-size tables for investigators to use.

This neglect of statistical power is not unique to the psychological and social science arenas. In exercise science, Baumgartner (1974), Christensen and Chris-

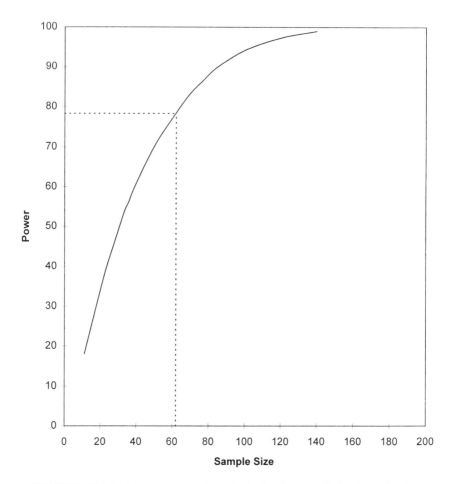

FIGURE 2 Relation between power and sample size based on t distribution (α = 5%, effect size = 0.50).

tensen (1977), Dotson (1980), Franks and Huck (1986), and Thomas, Salazar, and Landers (1991) have sounded warnings for investigators to attend to power, alpha level, and effect size when designing and interpreting research. Moher et al.'s (1994) recent study, published in the *Journal of the American Medical Association* (*JAMA*), examined this problem in the randomized controlled trial (RCT) literature. Moher et al. reviewed 383 RCTs published in *JAMA,* the *Lancet,* and the *New England Journal of Medicine* in the years 1975, 1980, 1985, and 1990. Of the 383 RCTs reviewed, 27% (n = 102) reported negative (statistically nonsignificant) results; of these, only 16% had at least 80% power to detect a 25% relative difference (Moher et al.'s measure of effect size). Further, only 32% (n = 33) reported a sample-size calculation. Compared to what Sedlmeier and Gigerenzer (1989) reported in the psychological literature, the power status of RCTs appears much better, although there is still much room for improvement.

Not surprisingly, Moher et al. (1994) recommended that all studies report sample-size calculations, including (a) primary outcome variable, (b) clinically important treatment effect, (c) absolute or relative status of this effect, and (c) statistical test, directionality, alpha level, and statistical power used to estimate sample size. What is not mentioned but implicit in these recommendations is that the estimation technique should be carefully matched to the experimental design.

This leads to the topic of this article—matching the design (i.e., repeated-measures ANOVA) with recent advances in sample-size calculations. Also, following Cohen's (1992) suggestion that "one possible reason for the continued neglect of statistical power analysis in research in the behavioral sciences is the inaccessibility of, or difficulty with, the standard material" (p. 155), my presentation in this article requires that the investigator do no more than read a table or examine a figure. (Those readers needing more details are directed to the references cited.) This, it is hoped, will lead readers to increase their use of sample-size estimation in future studies. Perhaps I should, like Cohen, check back in 30 years to see if readers of this journal have followed this advice!

METHODS FOR ESTIMATING SAMPLE SIZE AND RELATED POWER FOR REPEATED-MEASURES ANOVA

Importance of Accurate Sample-Size Estimation

When negative results occur in biomedical and other areas of research, and when sufficient sample sizes are available to detect clinically important effects, then the negative results are interpretable. With sufficient power, negative results imply that the intervention (treatment) did not have effects as large as those considered to be clinically meaningful. However, without sufficient power, a clinically important but statistically nonsignificant outcome may be ignored or (worse) taken to mean that the intervention made no difference. This is an example of a Type II error that, by definition, would be high given low power (power = $1 - \beta$).

Added to statistical reasons (i.e., Type II error; ability to make correct decisions) are ethical reasons for estimating sample size before conducting a study. Altman (1980) observed that trials with too many subjects or patients would unnecessarily incur additional financial costs and risk to patients; trials with too few patients would place patients at risk with little possibility of detecting clinically important differences. That is, an underpowered study would be "scientifically useless, and hence unethical in its use of subjects and other resources" (p. 1338).

Standard Estimation Techniques

Calculation of the minimum required sample size for adequate statistical power is one of the more important functions in preparation for a research effort. Typically, a sufficiently large sample is required to demonstrate clinically meaningful differences among the treatment groups according to prescribed specifications. To determine appropriate sample size for a repeated-measures ANOVA, two approaches are typically used (Rochon, 1991).

The first approach is to perform a univariate sample-size calculation based on the outcome expected at a single point in time; this approach ignores the structure in the repeated-measures protocol and, depending on the exact hypothesis of interest, might underestimate or overestimate the required sample size. The second approach is to "average" across the repeated measurements by dividing the variance anticipated at any time point by the number of repeated measurements; this approach ignores the correlation structure among the repeated measurements and typically underestimates the variance of the mean (Rochon, 1991).

Unfortunately, these two approaches also ignore one of the advantages of performing repeated measurements—the ability to consider a variety of hypotheses within the same study. The traditional statistical test for the main effect of the treatment evaluates treatment differences "averaged" across repeated measurements. Differences at specific points, or at every time point during the course of the trial, might also be tested. Or, the real interest may be the linear trend over time. Thus, repeated-measurement designs are particularly useful for investigating consistency in treatment effects over time.

When the dependent variable (outcome) is measured on a continuous scale and observed at a single point in time, sample-size calculation procedures are well established (Cohen, 1988; Fleiss, 1986). However, the corresponding situation for repeated-measures experiments is less well known. Under this design, subjects are randomly allocated to two or more treatment groups, and every subject is evaluated repeatedly at well-defined points in time during the course of the study. A correlation structure is assumed among the set of repeated measures captured from any individual, although the vectors of repeated measures from different subjects are considered to be independent. Surprisingly, little work has been performed to account for this correlation structure in planning repeated-measures experiments.

Review of Repeated-Measures Design

In a repeated-measurement design, several hypotheses can be tested. An important consideration is that each hypothesis has a different impact on the sample size needed for adequate power. This is due to the nature and utility of the hypothesis. Three possible hypotheses are considered—H_1, H_2, and H_3 (Rochon, 1991).

Hypothesis H_1.   For H_1, the Type I error rate is maintained at a prescribed alpha level for all comparisons, simple and complex. Thus, H_1 is appropriate when investigators propose a wide variety of hypotheses over the time course of the study. For example, treatment differences at one or more time points can be examined as well as comparisons between the change scores from one set of time points to another. Other "data-snooping" excursions into the data set can also be considered. As H_1 tests for equality at every time point (an extensive hypothesis), the "penalty" is a very conservative approach for controlling the overall Type I error rate (see Scheffé, 1959). The end result is that larger sample sizes (than H_2; see Table 1) will be required for adequate power.

Also appropriate under H_1 is when dimensions other than time underlie the repeated measurements. For instance, the dimension can be dosages of a drug treatment, where different doses are tested within the same group of subjects.

Hypothesis H_2. H_2 tests for treatment main effects (Cole & Grizzle, 1966). In contrast to H_1, which tests for differences at each time point (repeated measurements), H_2 compares the "average" across time points and groups. As such, H_2 is less demanding than H_1. Under otherwise equivalent conditions, H_2 results in smaller sample sizes than H_1 for adequate power (see Table 2). However, H_2 is based on the assumption that there is no Treatment × Time interaction. As a result, use of H_2 should be approached with some caution.

Hypothesis H_3. H_3 tests whether treatment differences are consistent from time point to time point. For example, if the first of several repeated measurements represents a baseline measure, then H_3 tests for equality of changes from baseline to each of the succeeding measurements (i.e., a gain-score analysis). In contrast to H_2, H_3 evaluates the Treatment × Time interaction. For studies in which interaction of this nature is anticipated, it is important to have sufficient power to detect clinically meaningful interactions. However, adequate power to detect interactions generally requires greater sample sizes (see Table 3) than equivalent conditions under H_2 (detection of main effects).

DISCUSSION

Estimation of Sample Size: *t* Test Versus Repeated-Measures ANOVA

Tables 1, 2, and 3 (calculated from equations provided in Rochon, 1991) show, for the repeated-measure ANOVA, the required sample size per group for 80% power (two-tailed $\alpha = 5\%$) for varying effect size, number of repeated measurements (T),

TABLE 1
Hypothesis H_1: Minimum Number of Subjects Required in Each Treatment Group for a
Two-Sided Test at $\alpha = 5\%$ and $\beta = 20\%$ for Selected Values of T, ρ, and Effect Size

T	ρ	Effect Size					
		0.1	0.3	0.5	0.7	0.9	1.1
3	0	729	83	32	17	12	9
	0.1	830	94	36	19	13	10
	0.2	937	106	40	22	14	10
	0.3	1,052	119	44	24	16	11
	0.4	1,177	133	49	27	17	12
	0.5	1,311	148	55	29	19	13
	0.6	1,456	164	61	32	21	15
	0.7	1,614	182	67	35	22	16
	0.8	1,787	201	74	39	25	17
	0.9	1,975	222	81	43	27	19
5	0	516	60	24	14	10	8
	0.1	604	70	27	16	11	9
	0.2	703	81	31	18	12	9
	0.3	817	94	36	20	14	10
	0.4	948	108	41	23	15	11
	0.5	1,103	125	47	26	17	13
	0.6	1,286	146	55	30	19	14
	0.7	1,507	170	63	34	22	16
	0.8	1,779	201	74	40	25	18
	0.9	2,123	239	88	47	30	21
7	0	414	50	21	13	10	8
	0.1	490	58	24	14	11	9
	0.2	578	68	27	16	12	9
	0.3	682	79	31	18	13	10
	0.4	808	93	36	21	14	11
	0.5	961	110	42	24	16	12
	0.6	1,152	132	50	28	19	14
	0.7	1,398	159	60	33	21	16
	0.8	1,726	195	73	39	26	19
	0.9	2,185	246	91	49	31	22
9	0	353	44	19	12	10	9
	0.1	420	51	22	14	11	9
	0.2	499	60	25	15	12	10
	0.3	594	70	29	17	13	10
	0.4	712	83	33	20	14	11
	0.5	858	100	39	23	16	12
	0.6	1,048	121	47	26	18	14
	0.7	1,303	149	57	31	21	16
	0.8	1,662	189	71	39	25	19
	0.9	2,207	249	93	50	32	23

TABLE 2

Hypothesis H_2: Minimum Number of Subjects Required in Each Treatment Group for a Two-Sided Test at $\alpha = 5\%$ and $\beta = 20\%$ for Selected Values of T, ρ, and Effect Size

		Effect Size					
T	ρ	0.1	0.3	0.5	0.7	0.9	1.1
3	0	525	60	22	12	8	6
	0.1	598	68	25	14	9	7
	0.2	678	77	29	15	10	7
	0.3	765	86	32	17	11	8
	0.4	860	97	36	19	12	9
	0.5	961	108	40	21	13	9
	0.6	1,069	120	44	23	15	10
	0.7	1,184	133	49	26	16	11
	0.8	1,306	146	54	28	18	12
	0.9	1,435	161	59	31	19	13
5	0	315	36	14	8	6	4
	0.1	370	42	16	9	6	5
	0.2	433	49	19	10	7	5
	0.3	508	58	22	12	8	6
	0.4	596	68	25	14	9	7
	0.5	700	79	29	16	10	7
	0.6	823	93	34	18	12	8
	0.7	968	109	40	21	13	10
	0.8	1,138	128	47	25	16	11
	0.9	1,338	150	55	29	18	13
7	0	226	26	11	6	5	5
	0.1	268	31	12	7	5	5
	0.2	318	37	14	8	6	5
	0.3	379	43	17	9	6	5
	0.4	454	52	20	11	7	5
	0.5	547	62	23	13	8	6
	0.6	665	75	28	15	10	7
	0.7	815	92	34	18	12	8
	0.8	1,007	113	42	22	14	10
	0.9	1,254	141	52	27	17	12
9	0	176	21	9	6	6	6
	0.1	210	25	10	6	6	6
	0.2	251	29	12	7	6	6
	0.3	302	35	14	8	6	6
	0.4	365	42	16	9	6	6
	0.5	447	51	19	11	7	6
	0.6	555	63	24	13	8	6
	0.7	701	79	29	16	10	7
	0.8	900	101	37	20	13	9
	0.9	1,179	132	49	26	16	11

TABLE 3
Hypothesis H$_3$: Minimum Number of Subjects Required in Each Treatment Group for a
Two-Sided Test at α = 5% and β = 20% for Selected Values of T, ρ, and Effect Size

		Effect Size					
T	ρ	*0.1*	*0.3*	*0.5*	*0.7*	*0.9*	*1.1*
3	0	3,856	430	156	81	50	34
	0.1	3,470	387	141	73	45	31
	0.2	3,085	345	125	65	40	28
	0.3	2,700	302	110	57	35	24
	0.4	2,314	259	95	49	31	21
	0.5	1,929	216	79	41	26	18
	0.6	1,544	173	64	34	21	15
	0.7	1,158	130	48	26	16	12
	0.8	773	88	33	18	12	9
	0.9	387	45	18	10	7	6
5	0	4,777	533	194	100	62	42
	0.1	4,300	480	175	91	56	38
	0.2	3,822	427	156	81	50	35
	0.3	3,345	374	137	71	44	31
	0.4	2,867	321	117	61	38	27
	0.5	2,390	268	98	52	32	23
	0.6	1,913	215	79	42	27	19
	0.7	1,435	162	60	32	21	15
	0.8	958	109	41	22	15	11
	0.9	480	56	22	13	9	7
7	0	5,453	609	222	115	71	49
	0.1	4,908	549	200	104	64	44
	0.2	4,363	488	178	93	58	40
	0.3	3,818	428	156	82	51	35
	0.4	3,273	367	134	70	44	31
	0.5	2,729	306	113	59	37	26
	0.6	2,184	246	91	48	31	22
	0.7	1,639	185	69	37	24	17
	0.8	1,094	125	47	26	17	13
	0.9	549	64	26	15	11	9
9	0	6,013	672	245	127	79	54
	0.1	5,412	605	221	115	71	49
	0.2	4,811	539	197	103	64	44
	0.3	4,211	472	173	90	56	39
	0.4	3,610	405	149	78	49	34
	0.5	3,009	338	125	66	42	29
	0.6	2,408	271	101	54	34	25
	0.7	1,807	205	77	41	27	20
	0.8	1,206	138	53	29	20	15
	0.9	605	71	29	17	12	10

and autocorrelation parameter (ρ, with $|\rho| < 1.0$). Table 4 (calculated from equations provided in Fleiss, 1986) shows, for the t-statistic model, the required sample size per group for 80% power (two-tailed $\alpha = 5\%$) for varying effect size (90% power and $\alpha = 1\%$ are also provided for the reader's use). Under equivalent conditions of power, alpha level, and effect size, required sample sizes vary according to class of hypothesis being tested (H_1, H_2, H_3, or t statistic), number of repeated measurements (T), and correlation among repeated measurements (ρ, with ρ interpretable as the correlation between any two adjacent repeated measures). The model described assumes an exponentially decreasing trend in the correlation pattern over time (Rochon, 1991).

Figure 3 shows the required sample sizes plotted against effect size for the four classes of hypotheses (H_1, H_2, H_3, t statistic) for "equivalent" conditions of power, alpha level, number of repeated measurements (T), and correlation among repeated measurements (ρ). It should be noted that differences in required sample sizes are most pronounced when effect size is small. That is, when clinically important effect size is hypothesized to be small, choosing the inappropriate class of hypothesis would result in large miscalculations of required sample sizes. If the t statistic is used as the basis for comparison (as it is typically used in the research literature), then, when the effect size is expected to be 0.30, the sample size requirement is 174 subjects per group. Comparable sample sizes for hypotheses H_1, H_2, and H_3 would be 148, 108, and 216, respectively. H_1 and H_2 show reduced sample-size requirements by 26 and 66 subjects per group. If, for a clinical trial, the assumed cost per subject or patient is approximately \$5,000, then up to \$660,000 ($2 \times 66 \times \$5,000$) would be saved by assuming H_2 instead of the t statistic. Other factors not included in the dollar amount would be time incurred and risk to patients.

In contrast, if H_3 is appropriate, then an additional 42 subjects per group (216 minus 174) would be needed to have adequate power to detect the hypothesized Treatment × Time interaction. Otherwise, the clinical trial would not have had

TABLE 4

Minimum Number of Subjects in Each Treatment Group for a Two-Sided Test at $\alpha = 5\%$ and 1% and $\beta = 20\%$ and 10% for Selected Values of Effect Size

		Effect Size												
α	β	*0.2*	*0.3*	*0.4*	*0.5*	*0.6*	*0.7*	*0.8*	*0.9*	*1.0*	*1.1*	*1.2*	*1.3*	*1.4*	*1.5*
5	20	393	174	98	63	44	32	25	19	16	13	11	9	8	7
	10	525	233	131	84	58	43	33	26	21	17	15	12	11	9
1	20	582	259	146	93	65	48	36	29	23	19	16	14	12	10
	10	741	329	185	119	82	61	46	37	30	25	21	18	15	13

Note.   Based on t distribution.

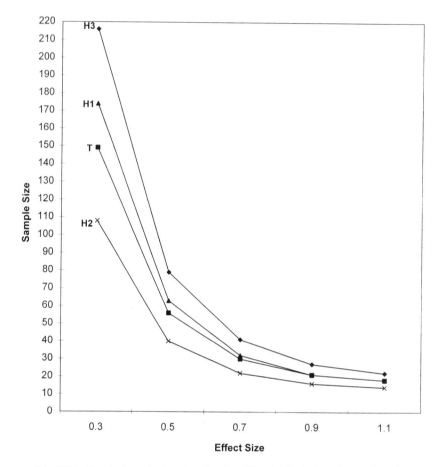

FIGURE 3 Required sample sizes plotted against effect size for the four classes of hypotheses for "equivalent" conditions of power (80%), alpha level (5%), number of repeated measurements (3), and correlation among repeated measurements ($\rho = .5$).

adequate power, and monetary and patient resources would have been wasted to run an underpowered trial.

Use of tables. Sample sizes for 80% power (two-tailed $\alpha = 5\%$) are determined for repeated-measures ANOVA from Tables 1, 2, and 3 as follows:

1. The effect size is the difference the investigator expects to find that would be considered clinically meaningful. Data to estimate this hypothesized effect can come from previous research, pilot data, or meta-analysis. To simplify the tables,

values included are in increments of 0.2 (i.e., 0.1, 0.3, etc.). For in-between values, say 0.4 or 0.8, it is appropriate to perform a linear interpolation between values. For example (see Figure 3, Table 1 with $T = 3$, $\rho = 0.5$), for H_1, sample size required for effect size 0.4 is approximately 102 (midway between 148 and 55). For effect size 0.8, sample size is approximately 24 (midway between 29 and 19). As the actual relation is nonlinear (Figure 3), the interpolated sample sizes are small overestimates of the actual sample sizes. The differences become smaller with larger effect sizes.

2. The number of repeated measures (T) is number of times a dependent variable is assessed. Thus, a study that includes baseline, midpoint, and final measurements would be $T = 3$.

3. The autocorrelation parameter ρ ($|\rho| < 1.0$) is the correlation among the repeated measurements and is interpretable as the correlation between any two adjacent repeated measures; ρ values can also be from previous research, pilot data, or meta-analysis. Thus, the intersection of effect size, T, and ρ gives the desired sample size.

Sample sizes for 80% and 90% power (two-tailed αs = 1% and 5%) are determined for a *t* test from Table 4. Table 4 is used by estimating the effect size as described in the previous paragraph. Two alpha levels (1% and 5%) and two power levels ($1 - \beta = 80\%$ and 90%) are provided in Table 4. Thus, the intersection of effect size and alpha level (for a given power level) gives the desired sample size.

SUMMARY AND CONCLUSION

Standard or usual techniques for estimating required sample sizes do not consider the correlation structure of the repeated-measures ANOVA. Thus, required sample size for a given design or for testing certain hypotheses might be overestimated or underestimated. In either case, monetary and human resources are wasted. Therefore, it is important from fiscal and ethical perspectives to match the design and hypothesis to the sample-size estimation technique.

ACKNOWLEDGMENTS

I thank Center for Research in Ambulatory Health Care Administration staff Tammy Blanc, Lisa Donovan, and Tom Richter for their invaluable contributions in preparing the manuscript and in its presentation at the 8th Measurement and

Evaluation Symposium, *Exploring the Kaleidoscope* (October 24 to 26, 1996, Oregon State University, Corvallis).

REFERENCES

Altman, D. G. (1980). Statistics and ethics in medical research: III. How large a sample? *British Medical Journal, 281,* 1336–1338.

Baumgartner, T. A. (1974). Remarks concerning sampling used in the *Research Quarterly. Research Quarterly, 45,* 215–216.

Christensen, J. E., & Christensen, C. E. (1977). Statistical power analysis of health, physical education, and recreation research. *Research Quarterly, 48,* 204–208.

Cohen, J. (1962). The statistical power of abnormal-social psychological research: A review. *Journal of Abnormal and Social Psychology, 65,* 145–153.

Cohen, J. (1969). *Statistical power analysis for the behavioral sciences.* New York: Academic.

Cohen, J. (1988). *Statistical power analysis for the behavioral sciences* (2nd ed.). Hillsdale, NJ: Lawrence Erlbaum Associates, Inc.

Cohen, J. (1992). A power primer. *Psychological Bulletin, 112,* 155–159.

Cole, J. W. L., & Grizzle, J. E. (1966). Applications of multivariate analysis of variance to repeated measures experiments. *Biometrics, 22,* 810–828.

Donner, A. (1984). Approaches to sample size estimation in the design of clinical trials—A review. *Statistics in Medicine, 3,* 199–214.

Dotson, C. O. (1980). Logic of questionable density. *Research Quarterly for Exercise and Sport, 51,* 23–36.

Fleiss, J. L. (1986). *The design and analysis of clinical experiments.* New York: Wiley.

Franks, B. D., & Huck, S. W. (1986). Why does everyone use the .05 significance level? *Research Quarterly for Exercise and Sport, 57,* 245–249.

Glass, G. V., McGaw, B., & Smith, M. L. (1981). *Meta-analysis in social research.* Beverly Hills, CA: Sage.

Hsieh, F. Y. (1989). Sample size tables for logistic regression. *Statistics in Medicine, 8,* 795–802.

Lachin, J. M. (1981). Introduction to sample size determination and power analysis for clinical trials. *Controlled Clinical Trials, 2,* 93–113.

Moher, D., Dulberg, C. S., & Wells, G. A. (1994). Statistical power, sample size, and their reporting in randomized controlled trials. *Journal of the American Medical Association, 272,* 122–124.

Rochon, J. (1991). Sample size calculations for two-group repeated-measures experiments. *Biometrics, 47,* 1383–1398.

Scheffé, H. (1959). *The analysis of variance.* New York: Wiley.

Sedlmeier, P., & Gigerenzer, G. (1989). Do studies of statistical power have an effect on the power of studies? *Psychological Bulletin, 105,* 309–316.

Stevens, J. (1992). *Applied multivariate statistics for the social sciences* (2nd ed.). Hillsdale, NJ: Lawrence Erlbaum Associates, Inc.

Thomas, J. R., Salazar, W., & Landers, D. M. (1991). What is missing in $p < .05$? Effect size. *Research Quarterly for Exercise and Sport, 62,* 344–348.

van Belle, G., & Martin, D. C. (1993). Sample size as a function of coefficient of variation and ratio of means. *American Statistician, 47,* 165–167.